W9-ADP-538

EAT IT!
food adventures with marco polo

VOLUME ONE:
leaving home

By Gracie Cavnar
with Illustrations by Anni Matsick

S2P Press

Houston, Texas

Jefferson Madison
Regional Library
Charlottesville, Virginia

30620 0211
A

Copyright © 2012 Gracie Cavnar

Illustrations by Anni Matsick
Additional Line Drawings by Edd Patton and Joshua Wilson
Book Design by Molly Cumming

Published by:

S2P Press is an imprint of Recipe for Success Foundation
P.O. Box 56405 Houston, Texas 77256
Phone: 713.520.0443 Fax: 713.520.0453

www.recipe4success.org/S2PPress

The story of Ottavio Fornero is entirely a work of fiction. While historic characters, places and events are incorporated; references to them are purely the product of the author's imagination. All rights reserved. No part of this book may be reproduced, stored in a retrieval system, or transmitted in any form or by any means without written permission from the publisher except by a reviewer who may quote brief passages or reproduce illustrations in a review with appropriate credits.

FIRST EDITION
Manufactured in the United States of America

Library of Congress Cataloging-in-Publication Data Library of Congress Control Number: 2012913326

Cavnar, Gracie
    Eat It! Food Adventures with Marco Polo, Volume One: Leaving Home / Gracie Cavnar
    1. Cookery, children   2. Marco Polo, Juvenile fiction   3. Recipe for Success Foundation
    (organization)   4. Childhood Obesity   I. Title

ISBN 978-0-9846525-0-1

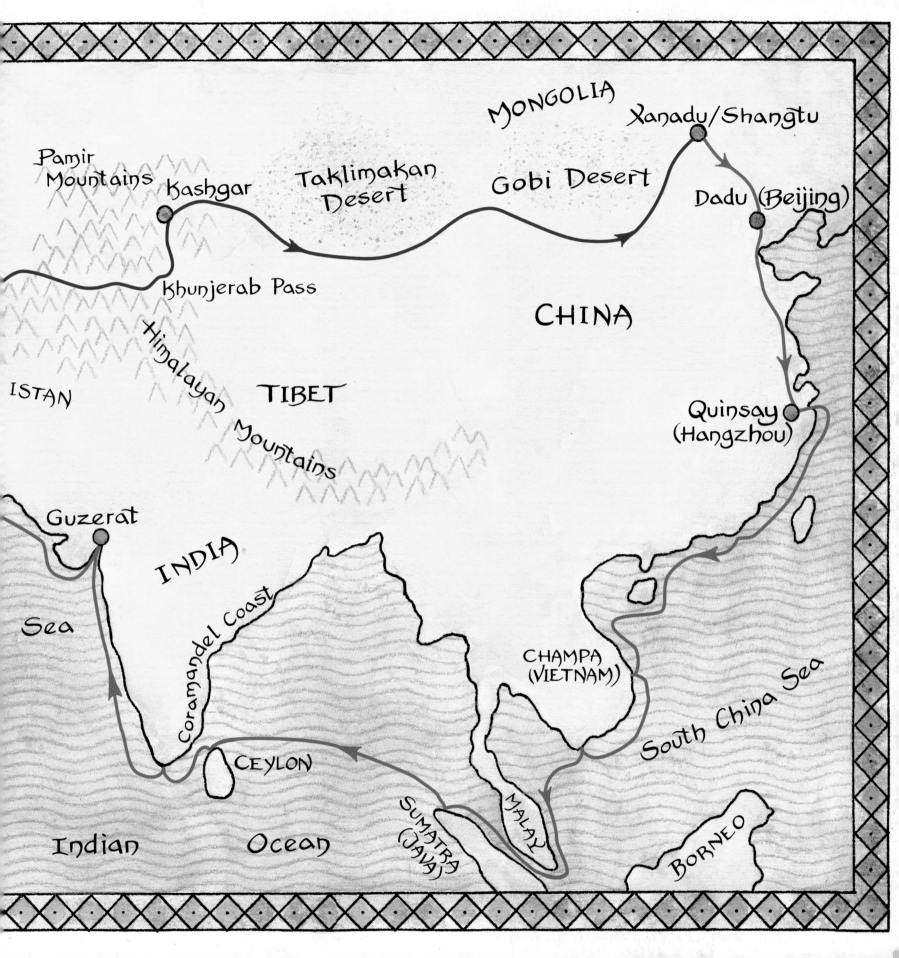

to my husband, children & grandchildren

"life is an adventure"

NOTE FROM THE AUTHOR

Food has been at the center of our lives since the dawn of mankind. It was food that drove us from our caves to explore the world. Food fueled trade, motivated curiosity, invention, travel and wars. Food was even responsible for the discovery of America. Columbus was in search of spices for a demanding European palate, not a new continent. Life revolves around the availability of food and the capricious weather cycles that govern it. A new industry emerged after World War II that used science and technology in an attempt to harness nature and smooth the bumps between feast and famine. Now, there are more than 10,000 new processed food products introduced to the market each year; reality television has turned cooking into entertainment; and we are eating ourselves silly. There have been unintended consequences.

For generations, family traditions and our best childhood memories have centered on food. But sadly in the 21st century, many of us have lost our connection to real food, its source and history. What happens when we subtract awareness and traditional meaning from food and take away the wonderful gift of having time to sit for daily meals with our friends and family? Besides a loss of culture and social bonding, we now see how this disconnection has triggered waves of unhealthy effects ripping through our society, the most prevalent of these being obesity and the chronic diseases that result from it.

In the mid-nineties, to help turn back the unprecedented surge of childhood obesity, we launched programs to reach out to children and reconnect them with real, unprocessed food. This book is an extension of that effort. We know that children are willing to eat just about anything they grow or cook, and our Seed-to-Plate Nutrition Education™ programs at Recipe for Success Foundation that teach them how, have helped establish lifelong healthy habits. To our delight, we discovered that children also like the stories and rituals that surround food, which presented us with another teaching moment:

Understanding our neighbors and enriching our lives by planning, preparing and enjoying our meals together.

My family lives in a melting pot of a city filled with people from hundreds of countries, which offers unlimited opportunity for food adventures. Our global village is just a microcosm of America, an immigrant nation with a rich tapestry of culinary traditions. *Eat It! Food Adventures with Marco Polo* is the first in a series of children's books aimed at exploring the history of what we eat. I hope it inspires you to have an adventure of your own, to make these recipes together as a family, maybe even to launch some new traditions, but most of all to have fun with your food.

Gracie Cavnar
@graciecavnar

ACKNOWLEDGEMENTS

My deepest gratitude goes to The Robert and Janice McNair Foundation and Sara S. Morgan for their generosity towards underwriting this book. And many thanks to the collaborators who contributed, including: my son Justin, who was my first proving ground; Recipe for Success Foundation Staff Chefs, who tested, tested, tested— Veronica Alford, Carolyn Carcasi, Molly Kaminski and Mark Wilson; founding members of Recipe for Success Foundation's Chefs Advisory Board, who inspired me with their enthusiasm and recipes—Robert DelGrande, Randy Evans, Lance Fegan, Allan King, and Monica Pope; my intrepid volunteer editor, Anita Garten and proofreader, Cathi Walsh; my amazing friend Molly Cumming who cooked, coached and crafted this beautiful book into existence; friends in Houston, Texas, and Woodstock, Vermont, whose children tested and tasted every recipe from the perspective of 4-12 year old cooks, including the Casberian, Eastman, Lackley and Walker families; and the thousands of children who participate in Recipe for Success Foundation programs. It's the children who continually motivate me with their eagerness to find magic in the garden and kitchen, and reignite my passion for great food that is connected to place. Now, let's cook!

FOREWARD

At seventeen, I already knew I wanted to be a chef. After apprenticeships and stints in many restaurants around the world then owning and operating three of my own in Houston, I've enjoyed many delicious successes, tasted a little failure and even had a brief stint as a reality TV star on Bravo's "Top Chef's Masters." I've learned one important lesson: Food is a journey.

My own food journey started when I was about Tavi's age, because I wanted to find out who I was, who my family was, where we came from and how we cooked. Really, I wanted to hear stories. And that's why I was so excited for the opportunity to write the foreword for this amazing cookbook, *Eat it! Food Adventures with Marco Polo*.

At its heart, this book is a about the powerful way that food affects our lives and the world around us. It is a journey, not just of food discovery, but self-discovery. Through the lens of Tavi and his friend Marco Polo, readers—young and old alike—learn about exotic food and spices and the cultural traditions of dining in faraway lands and come to realize how much fun it is to share these finds with family and friends around their own table. It's poignant when Tavi appreciates that he misses his mother's cooking and understands how profoundly she influenced him with her stories, her sense of adventure and her gift for creating wonderful meals. He only wishes he had paid closer attention to how she cooked. Then Tavi realizes he may have inherited her gift after all with his "nose" and enthusiasm for good, real food—a talent that may help him begin to craft his own story.

This wonderful book is an outgrowth of the fabulous work of the Recipe for Success Foundation, which Gracie started in 2005 (and soon after enticed my help). The Recipe for Success Foundation's mission is to combat childhood obesity through dynamic, interactive programs that bring chefs (like me) and gardens into schools to help kids learn that eating well is both easy and fun.

Each school year, many of the children we teach begin with a slim connection to food: It's something that comes from a drive-through, or a can, or a take-out box. We have touched thousands of kids, cooking and gardening with them, bringing their connection to food alive with real experiences in the kitchen and at the table and inspiring them to write wonderful stories about their own family's food traditions. And *voila*! Somewhere along the way, they become thoughtful, informed, curious eaters and cooks. Every year, even though I know it is going to happen, this transformation continues to astound and move me. Kids just get it when they're involved in the whole experience. And as this book takes the lessons we've learned from the classroom into your home, I hope it will move you too.

Food is the language of family and the spice—the extra touch that make food taste fantastic—are the stories. This book has a wonderful story and fantastic recipes and tools to help any young person begin their own journey—just as I did many years ago—to discover where they come from and who they are. I hope it inspires you to reconnect with family and community around the table with good food. With deep delight, I know you will enjoy this book with your family and the food journey it takes all of you on.

Monica Pope
Chef and owner, Sparrow Bar + Cookshop
@MonicaPope

TABLE *of* CONTENTS

THE ADVENTURE

CHAPTER 1: SETTING THE SCENE FOR ADVENTURE 17

CHAPTER 2: EXPECT THE UNEXPECTED 23

CHAPTER 3: THE PARTY 27

CHAPTER 4: SETTING SAIL 33

           EXPLORING THE GALLEY 36

CHAPTER 5: LIFE ABOARD THE SHIP 39

CHAPTER 6: THE FOOD GETS BETTER 43

RECIPES FROM VENICE TO GREECE

FLATBREAD & BEYOND 51

    Pancakes 52

    Basic Whole Wheat Flatbread 54

    Easy Focaccia 56

    Traditional Focaccia Genovese 58

    Pita 60

    Rustic Mushroom Tarts 62

PASTA & RICE 65

    Basic Fresh Pasta Dough 66

    Losyns 70

    Traditional Pesto 72

    Za'atar Style Pesto 73

    Pasta Primavera 74

    Radishes & Greens with Pasta 76

    Ravioli with Fresh Herbs 78

    Artichokes & Orzo 80

    Asparagus Risotto 82

PROTEINS AND VEGGIES 84

    Stuffed Eggs 86

    Barley & Lentil Soup 88

    Walnuts in Brussels 90

    Roasted Vegetables with Gremolata 92

    Spring Salad in Bloom 94

    Homemade Yogurt 96

    Greek Yogurt 97

    Tzatziki 98

    Kalamaki 100

    Feta & Veggie Roll-ups 102

    Fish Soup 104

DESSERTS 107

    Pears & Cinnamon 108

    Saffron & Fig Cake 110

    Fruit & Honey Bundles 112

    Yiaourti Me Meli 114

THE EXTRAS

    Where Did This Come From? 116

    A Note About Flour and Bread 128

    Kitchen Rules 132

    How Much Is This? (Measurements Explained) 133

    Kitchen Stuff (Illustrated Tools) 134

    How Do I? (Illustrated Techniques) ...138

    Cooking Terms 142

INDEX 148

ABOUT THE AUTHOR 156

the adventure

chapter 1

SETTING THE SCENE FOR ADVENTURE

It started off like any other day. Marco Polo and Tavi Fornero sat in the third floor drawing room of the Fornero villa playing chess. Tavi distractedly ran his hand through his thick black curly hair before picking up his white knight and moving it up two squares in front of his pawn. "I see what you are up to," grinned Marco as he moved his own knight two places.

The soft morning sun streamed in through the room's three tall windows. They were open with their heavy drapes pulled back, allowing the fresh air and city hubbub to drift up from below. The boys could hear the gondoliers calling to each other as they poled their long boats through the canals. Low whispers of neighbors lingering to gossip were punctured by "*buongiorno!*" from people bustling by. Tavi felt very happy. Everything in his world was finally perfect again. It would be more perfect if he managed to beat Marco today, so he tried to ignore the noise and concentrate on his next move.

Marco had been his tutor for six years, four hours a day, six days a week. When Tavi's father died three years ago, they started spending even more time together. Though he was only eleven and Marco nearly seventeen, they were closer than brothers. Marco let Tavi tag along everywhere with him, like a special helper. They liked to do a lot of the same stuff like draw maps and read about far away places. Marco encouraged Tavi to daydream about traveling to all the places on their maps and to write down his fantasy stories, which transformed the drudgery of lessons into play. Tavi's real brothers were too busy to play. They made fun of his dreams and called him *mammoni*, a Mama's boy.

Although they were just getting to know him, Marco's father was an excellent source of information and inspiration for stories. Niccolò Polo was a famous Venetian trader. He left on an epic journey before Marco was even born and didn't come back for fifteen years! Suddenly he appeared eighteen months ago, with silk and spices and wondrous tales of adventures in faraway places. He was a celebrity. Tavi and Marco couldn't get enough of him, and they hung around his warehouse asking endless questions: "What does a camel look like? Does it bite you? What is a desert? What does snow taste like? Tell us about the Kublai Khan! Is he a scary man?"

In Tavi's favorite imaginary adventures, he was a valiant champion. He saved the day and brought home treasure to Mama, returning to Venice a celebrity, like Marco's father. He entertained Mama with his yarns. She

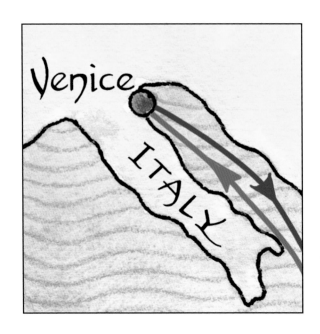

always laughed, and called him her brave hero. He liked that.

Just then, his Mama walked in the door like a breath of fresh air. She was a very handsome woman. Everyone said so. She was regal with her blonde hair elegantly pulled back, but she had a loving smile and kind face. Seeing her made Tavi feel warm and cozy, like someone had just put a blanket over his shoulders.

"Hello boys," she smiled. "I see that we are hard at work on our lessons."

"Papà says that playing chess is a good way to learn how to think," said Marco. "So, I am teaching Tavi the game. He's a fast learner." Tavi grinned at them both and moved his bishop. "Maybe too fast!" Marco laughed, shaking his head. "Hey, you'll never believe what my Papà told me last night," Marco said, as he moved his pawn. "He has to go back to China to see the Kublai Khan, and he's thinking about taking me with him. How about that?"

Tavi felt every bit of blood drain from his face. He shivered, suddenly ice cold; dumbstruck. The thought of Marco leaving was more than he could bear. He took a slow, deep breath, trying hard to hide his anxiety and said, "How exciting that will be! You are so lucky!"

"I'm not having much luck with this game!" laughed Marco. "Fortunately, you will have to wait until tomorrow to beat me. I have to go now." He continued, "For today's assignment, Tavi, I want you to write a report about Venetian commerce." Tavi was distracted and didn't seem to hear. Ignoring his mood, Marco said, "Remember our lesson? You will have to stop thinking about chess and get to work on your real studies." Marco bowed to *signora* Fornero and hurried out the door.

Tavi remained at the table, his chin on his hands, staring glumly out the window. His oldest brother, Philipe walked in and cocked his head "What is he moping around about?" he asked.

"Marco was talking about going away with his father on a trip," Mama said.

"Ottavio Fornero, why do you even believe that Marco? He is just making up stories like the ones you make up all the time," Philipe snorted. "You need to quit with the daydreaming and start thinking about going to work in one of the family businesses. Just pick one and let me get you started. Otherwise you will be a *mammoni* forever, holding on to Mama's apron strings."

Philipe picked up an apple, tossed it in the air, caught it and took a bite as he strode out of the room. Tavi made a face to his back. He was just about sick of all seven of his older brothers and their taunts.

"Don't worry Tavi, it's good to dream," Mama consoled him, "all great men dream."

"But I never dreamed that Marco would leave me!" Tavi cried. He couldn't hold it in a minute longer. "Mama, when do you think they will go? I wish I could go, too! Will I be old enough by then?"

"Oh, sweet one," soothed Mama. "You will make yourself crazy thinking this way. Let's just see what happens. It could be years away, and you might be surprised at how things change. Now, why don't you run an errand for me? Getting outside in the fresh air will clear your head. I need ricotta and mozzarella cheese, plus cinnamon and nutmeg. Now off you go!"

Mama had a way of cheering him up. She was right. He was happy to escape the house. Tavi sang Mama's list as he raced out the door. "Get my spice and cheese, if you please!" The minute he crossed the threshold, his dreams flickered back on in full color. He smiled at the sunny day that greeted him. "I'll be a trader when I grow up," he reassured himself. "I am not going to be trapped in some office, or shop, or bakery my whole life like my brothers. I will see the world, like Marco Polo's father!"

Tavi knew his life would change forever with Marco gone. He would be so lonely. "There's no one left who understands me like Marco does. But Mama said I would be surprised how things can change. I wonder what she

meant by that?" mused Tavi. "No! I'm not going to think about it today. Like Mama said, it could be years before the Polos leave again. Right now I'm on my way to the Rialto market." He loved to go to the Rialto. The spicy smells and exotic-looking merchants reminded him of Niccolò Polo's stories.

Tavi ran as fast as he could, away from sad thoughts and through the people jostling along the narrow passages. "Venice is getting so big. Mama says we're going to sink! I wonder if that's true," he thought. Marco told him that there were more than 80,000 people living there. Tavi started making a mental list of facts for the report he needed write.

"It's 1271, Tavi," Marco said during their lessons last week. "Venice isn't just a bunch of families living on lagoons anymore. We are the commercial capital of Europe." Thinking of this made Tavi proud to be a Venetian. He started looking around for other interesting things to put in his report.

He loved his hometown, and he knew it like the back of his hand. Instead of streets, there were canals. Most people used special boats called gondolas to get from one place to another. The gondoliers sang as they navigated their slender craft using long poles to push through the water. The canals were crisscrossed with a web of footbridges and bordered with narrow sidewalks connected by a maze of back allies. Away from the canals, the passages were dark, because they were lined with tall stone villas that blocked the sun. To get around without a gondola, Tavi had to maneuver through the dark alleys. Suddenly he stepped into *Piazza San Marco*, a huge sunlit square. He flapped his arms and flew across the plaza right through the middle of hundreds of black birds, laughing with delight when they took off all at once in a big commotion.

"Bzzeek, bzzeek!" he yelled as he soared, mimicking the panicked birds. Looming on one side of the square was the gold-domed basilica, huge, imposing and guarded by four gigantic, golden horses that glittered in the sun. Mama told him that the horse statues were stolen from Constantinople during a war. Tavi liked the sound of that far off place. "Constantinople, kon-stan-te-no-pel," he repeated to himself, "I wonder if everything there is gold. Maybe someday I can see for myself."

On the far side of the plaza, Tavi plunged back into a labyrinth of cobblestone alleys. He crossed over six little canals on small jiggly rope bridges, being careful to keep his balance. Finally he came to the big, new wooden Rialto Bridge that spanned the enormous Grand Canal. The marvelous bridge could break in half and open up like a present to allow ships to pass underneath. "Something for my report," he thought. On the other side of the bridge was the sprawling Rialto market. It bustled with hundreds of people who milled around the endless shops and stalls that were packed side by side in rows that stretched forever. Tavi started to run across the bridge but stopped halfway to get a good look below. He didn't want to miss anything he could turn into a story for Mama or use in his report for Marco. He breathed in the mysterious perfumes and let the sounds of dozens of languages and the sights of colorful, strange clothes and foreign faces engulf him as he gazed down.

There, floating in the Grand Canal was a massive galley with dozens of pennants gaily flying from its masts. The Captain stood high up in the prow and shouted orders to men who carried big bundles, jars, trunks and barrels from the Rialto up the ship's gangplank. In the back, on the tall poop deck, stood two very well-dressed Venetian men, talking and looking at a map. "Wait!" Tavi recognized them. "It's Marco's father and uncle! Oh no! Are they preparing for their trip, already?" He panicked, asking no one in particular, "is Marco really going this time?" Tavi's heart sank.

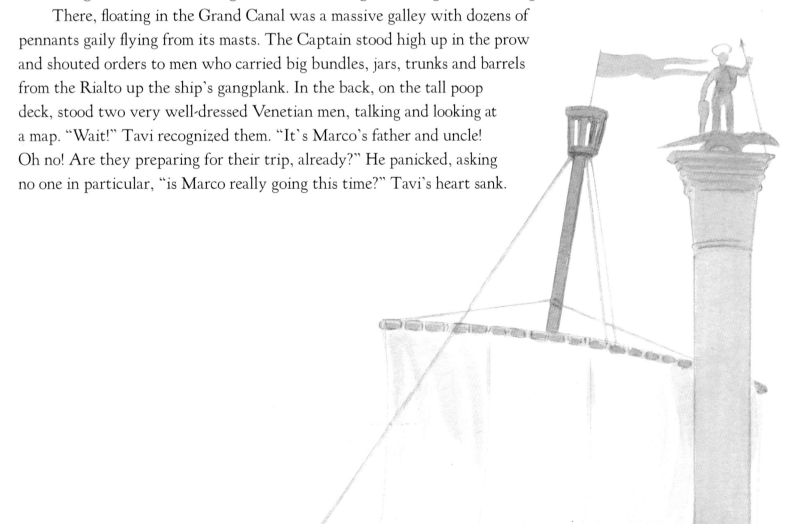

chapter 2

EXPECT THE UNEXPECTED

"Mama! Mama!" Tavi sobbed as he raced into his house. "He's leaving me." He practically knocked Mama down as he threw his arms around her waist and buried his head in her skirts.

She gently patted his back. "Come now, my sweet. Who is leaving you?"

"M-M-Mar-co! He has to be because he said he was probably going with his father next time and there in the canal I saw them on a galley getting ready go I know it oh what will I do I will be all alone now with no one to play chess with or to teach me things and once he said that we would be explorers together someday but I know he was just talking they will never take me," Tavi howled.

"Now, now," Mama hugged him, "calm down. Besides, you're smooshing my cheese."

"Uh-oh. The cheese." Tavi was so upset when he saw the ship, that he ran all the way home from the Grand Canal without even stopping to buy the things his mother had sent him to get. "I'm so sorry," he pleaded. "I forgot."

"Tavi!" She lifted his chin up gently to look straight into his brown eyes. They were swimming with tears. "*Mi amore*, you knew this might happen. Probably Marco would love for you to go, but I wouldn't get my hopes up for this time. His father might feel like one boy is enough to have along on such a journey. Someday . . ."

Everyone on an expedition has an important role. So, while Marco and his father are gone you can think about what your job might be and become very good at it. Then you will be as indispensable to them as you are to me. And you will get to go the next time. There will always be the next time.

Now, pull yourself together. I need you to go right back to the Rialto and get my ingredients. Afterwards, we will plan a proper send-off for Marco."

"OK Mama," Tavi sighed and hung his head as he walked out the door.

This time, he did not sing. He did not fly with the birds. He did not make up stories about the people he saw along the way. He couldn't stop crying as he trudged all the way back to the Rialto. Mama said he had to pull himself together, and he knew she was right. He couldn't let his brothers catch him crying. For sure he couldn't cry in front of Marco and his father.

"I don't want Marco to remember me blubbering away like a baby!" he decided, as he smeared away tears.

He found the stall of his mother's favorite cheese maker. "*Buongiorno, signore.* Mama needs ricotta and mozzarella today," he said.

"*Naturalmente!* Only the best for *signora* Fornero! You mean ricotta salata, correct? It's what she likes," the *vendora* said. Nodding, Tavi concentrated on his task as he inspected the creamy white cheese. It was drier than regular ricotta. He pinched a little off the big block to smell it. Then he rubbed the cheese between his fingers before popping it in his mouth and rolling it around on his tongue for a taste, just like Mama taught him.

"It should be nutty, a little bit sweet and have a crumbly texture," he remembered Mama saying. This was perfect. "I'll take a *pondera*," he told the man. "Ricotta cheese tastes so good," he thought, "especially mixed with the spices Mama uses, the nutmeg and cinnamon. But I like mozzarella, too." Tavi lingered to watch the cheese maker kneading a creamy ball. He stretched and pulled until it was shiny and then twirled it into long loops to make mozzarella. "That looks like it would be fun to do," Tavi said, and the cheese maker smiled and nodded. Tavi bought two of the coiled loops and thought about the cheese maker's job. "Is it indispensable?" he wondered.

His next stop was the apothecary shop to buy Mama's spices. The mustachioed merchant took whole round nutmegs and long rolls of cinnamon bark from their jars. Then he used a mortar and pestle to grind them into fine powders. While Tavi waited and watched, he noticed that the merchant's long, thin fingers were stained dark rust. "Probably from handling spices all day," thought Tavi. "I wonder if he has ever seen the places that his spices come from—Java, Ceylon and Sumatra. Marco has shown all of them to me on his maps."

A small vial of golden threads glittering on a high shelf caught Tavi's eye. "Saffron," he said, recognizing it. He knew that Greek farmers on the Island of Rhodes carefully pulled the tiny orange pistils from the centers of purple crocus flowers. The threads might be delicate, but they carried a powerful punch. Just one of them could flavor an entire dish. Saffron was so aromatic that ladies even used it in perfume. He remembered all this from one of Marco's lessons last year. "I'll take the whole vial," Tavi declared, pointing up to the shelf. It was expensive, but he knew Mama would like it. "I guess I'm trying to cheer myself up by making Mama happy," he thought. "I hope it works." Cinnamon and nutmeg and saffron all came to Venice by galley, just like the one Marco was leaving on.

"I'm not thinking about galleys and Marco right now. I have everything Mama asked for plus a little gift." The thought of pleasing Mama lifted his spirits, and he looked around the market for something else that might surprise her. One stall, covered by a bright blue and white awning, was packed with baskets of spring asparagus—green, white and purple. They looked like a thousand fingers with very pointy nails. "Perfect!" Tavi exclaimed as he picked up a dozen slender stalks. He haggled over the price and carefully counted out his coins.

The sun was low in the hazy sky, and it was getting late by the time Tavi hurried back across the Rialto Bridge. He tried to keep his mind off of Marco's departure, but he couldn't resist looking one last time at the loaded ship. Its sails were rolled down tight, and it was riding low in the water, heavy with cargo.

"It is also loaded with the adventures that lay ahead for my best friend," Tavi thought, "adventures that I won't get to share." He ducked his head and rushed on, fighting back tears.

POW! He ran headlong right into a very old, sunburned man who carried two baskets connected by a leather strap and slung over his shoulders. The man and his baskets tumbled to the ground.

"Pardon!" Tavi said, embarrassed as he rushed to help. "I am so sorry! But, what are these?" He held up four spongy little yellow and brown things. They looked like tiny tables.

"Wild mushrooms," the annoyed man replied as he gathered himself and tried to shoulder his baskets again. Tavi couldn't resist giving them the smell test.

"Mmm, mmm! Like the forest. May I buy some?" Tavi scooped up four double-hands full and added them to his rucksack. Moments later, he burst triumphantly through his front door, this time loaded with packages. "Mama, look at what I found!" He presented his surprise treasures to her: The crisp new asparagus, like a bouquet of spring flowers; the exotic saffron, like a precious gem; and the handfuls of mushrooms, like nuggets of valuable gold. He carefully laid them all out on the kitchen table alongside the cheeses and spices. Just as he suspected, Mama was gleeful.

"I've got a surprise for you, too," she said, clapping her hands. "The Polo family is coming to supper tomorrow night!"

"Good work Mama! Marco will never want to leave Venice if it means no more of your wonderful meals!" teased Tavi, trying to sound carefree so his mother wouldn't worry about him. But deep down inside he knew that this would be his last and only chance to convince Niccolò Polo to take him, too. How in the world would he do that? He had twenty-four hours to think of something.

chapter 3

THE PARTY

"It feels like today has lasted a lifetime," Tavi whined.

"Isn't it funny how when you are anxious for something to happen, the time oozes out like thick molasses?" said Mama, as she inspected her dining table. It was four meters long, covered to the floor in indigo silk that was embroidered with hunting scenes. On top was a white linen cloth. Three heavy, silver candlesticks commandeered the middle, and places arranged for twenty guests rimmed the edge. At each place, brilliant, gold-flecked, red glasses glittered next to softly gleaming pewter plates. To the side of each plate were an ivory-handled knife and a silver fork.

"Tell me about the forks again!" Tavi loved to hear stories about his Papà.

"Your Papà was always full of ideas," Mama laughed. "His *nonno* used to tell him about a Doge's wife, long ago, a Byzantine princess who used a fork at table. She was very unpopular. Venetians thought her haughty manners—using forks, finger bowls and napkins, were preposterous. Papà said that must be the only reason that forks didn't catch on back then, because he thought them very practical. He had one made for my twentieth birthday. That was before you were born. I liked it very much, but I soon realized that my fork was more than a gift. Papà was testing it on me!" Mama shook her head, remembering.

"And then Papà started making and selling them, right?" interrupted Tavi. "He used to say to me, 'Forks will be the next big thing.' Seems to me like all the Fornero businesses have something to do with food," he laughed. "Now, our Fornero's forks are considered the height of Venetian sophistication."

"Yes, your brothers plan to expand the business to all of Europe," Mama said with a note of pride in her voice.

Tavi considered the table that dominated the room and thought, "Every important event in my family has happened around this table—announcements, celebrations and parties, but I really like our regular meals the best." Regular Fornero meals were big, lively midday dinners and light evening suppers, when the whole family gathered, told stories and discussed the news and gossip of the day. Even though many of his brothers had their own families and now lived nearby instead of with Mama, this table was still the center of their lives.

He leaned against Papà's chair and slipped into the memory of another night around this table, when he was eight years old. It had been just months before Papà died so unexpectantly, and he was full of enthusiasm. "We are going to start baking and selling bread," he had announced as gasps raced around the table. "Nephew! This isn't done!" shouted Tavi's *grande zio*. "You will disgrace the family name. We are merchants and land owners, not bakers."

Papà just laughed. "I don't think it's disgraceful. After all, dear *zio*, don't we already have the ovens? What's wrong with putting them to work?"

"It's true," he answered, "but that's a Venetian tradition. Landlords operate free ovens for our tenants. We don't bake the bread ourselves, like servants."

Papà turned and spoke directly to Tavi then, like there was no one else in the room. "Remember son, you can't see if you don't look! We must always keep an eye open to new opportunities." Then he spun around to his elder. "Things change, *zio*. Travelers from all over the world come to Venice, but not always with their households along. They need to eat, and they will pay for great bread. We have ovens, and our staff can make it for us. We will still be merchants. Merchants of bread!"

When Tavi thought of Papà's mischievous smile that night, he felt a tingle run up his spine, and the fuzz on his arms prickled. The moment was seared into his memory, into his very soul, like the "F" they now burned into the Fornero bread loaves. He missed his Papà so much.

He shook off the dream and walked over to the dining room's tall window. It opened like a door onto a shallow balcony filled with red flowers. Tavi squeezed in between the flowerpots and leaned out over the lacy iron railing. The sky began to turn pink and orange, and he craned his neck around the shutters to see as far as he could in the fading light. He wanted to spot the Polo gondola when it first appeared around the bend of the canal.

"I haven't been able to think of a plan, but I do not want to wait for the next trip. I need to be indispensable now." His stomach filled with butterflies. They fluttered all the way up into his throat until he thought he would choke. Tavi considered his Papà's advice to keep his eyes open. "I would give anything to be like Papà, to make him proud. I practice keeping my eyes open all the time. So far I've only found saffron," he sighed. "How can I convince Niccolò Polo that I can see opportunities, too?" Mama came back into the dining room, and he twisted around to see what she was carrying. She and her cooks had been busy all day, so Tavi could guess with one sniff, but he asked anyway, "Mama, what are we having for supper tonight?"

"Stuffed eggs, fish soup, tarts made with those beautiful mushrooms," she smiled at him, "sweet pears cooked with cinnamon, raviolis filled with minced herbs and spices, a salad with lettuces and violet flowers, asparagus risotto," holding up a platter, she continued "and your favorite—losyns! Then for dessert, saffron cake." Tavi could tell that Mama was pleased with the menu. It was no wonder! It all sounded delicious, but his mouth actually watered with anticipation of the losyns. He knew that Mama had two secrets for perfect losyns: cinnamon and a hot oven.

"Mmm, I can taste the crusty cheese now, singeing my tongue. I love those layers of flavor," he said. He took a deep breath and let the aromas wash over him, mixing and mingling. His butterflies calmed down, and he laughed, "Thank goodness for our ovens." Mama nodded and twitched her nose.

People always remarked that Tavi's olive skin and dark curls favored his Papà, but he had his Mama's nose. He wished that it was more than looks they were talking about. Because just by using her nose, Mama could magically combine flavors and tastes so wonderfully that everyone swooned over the results. She didn't work in the kitchen herself. Mama had a legion of cooks and bakers who did that. But with Papà gone, she took over the family businesses and stuck her nose in everywhere. Tavi couldn't help but think that Mama was their new bakery's magic ingredient. The Forneros specialized in making focaccia, which was a traditional flatbread from Genoa drizzled with olive oil and sprinkled with rosemary and sea salt. But Mama instructed the cooks to add toppings like nuts, herbs, spices, cheese, vegetables and even sweet fruits. No one else did this. Fornero Focaccia was an instant hit. The family became famous for it, and his brothers had yet another booming business to manage. "Just as Papà predicted," remembered Tavi. Venetians started calling their street *Calle del Forno*, which means street of the oven.

Mama insisted that Tavi had her magic, too. He wondered, "If I really do have a magic nose, then maybe I could put it to good use in an indispensable way for this trip." But he was skeptical, "I probably need something more practical."

Suddenly he heard waves lapping against the house and turned back to the window to see the tip of the Polo's gondola appear. "They are here!" he shouted over his shoulder as he raced down the stairs, dizzyingly fast. He waited at the Fornero dock as the gondolier poled over to it. Marco jumped up next to Tavi, and the two of them helped Niccolò and his brother Maffeo step out. Niccolò had a very large map rolled up and tucked under his arm.

"Tavi, how did you know we were here?" he laughed good-naturedly. "Can you see around corners? That could be a handy talent!"

"I try to be helpful," Tavi said and led them upstairs to the *piano nobile*, the second floor of his house. The dining room was filling with Forneros gathering for the party: Mama, his *grande zio*, all his brothers, four of his brothers' wives, and several nieces and nephews.

"*Benvenuto*," said Mama as their guests made a slight bow to the ladies and kissed the men on each cheek. "Welcome! Niccolò! Maffeo! We are eager to hear about your expedition!" said Philipe. "Come have some wine and tell us, any opportunity for your old friends?"

"Well, let's take a look," said Niccolò. He unfurled his large map, and everyone crowded around to see it.

chapter 4

SETTING SAIL

"Am I dreaming?" whispered Tavi. He was in a fog. He tried to stay calm and focus as his family swirled around him like a tornado. "Pay attention!" he thought. "Don't miss anything."

The party seemed like a lifetime ago. He still couldn't believe his luck. All evening, both Marco and Mama were intent on pointing out Tavi's special talents to the Polo brothers. Marco bragged on his quick grasp of the finer strategies of chess and his keen observation skills. Mama went on and on about how he was always finding interesting new ingredients for her. She deflected every compliment for the meal. "Tavi discovered these mushrooms." or "Tavi found this saffron for me." After dessert, Niccolò pushed back his chair and announced, "Tavi, I think you could be very helpful on our expedition, if your Mama will let you come." Tavi nearly fainted.

The last two days were a blur of preparation. Now here he was in front of the Doge's palace saying goodbye to his family. They stood between the towering *Colonnes di Marco e Teodoro* that framed the broad plaza on the edge of the Grand Canal. The sun wasn't even up, and already the Forneros were just a small storm within a huge whirlwind of revelers. It seemed that all of Venice crowded the plaza to send-off the convoy. A dazzling pageantry of trumpets announced the arrival of the Doge and the aristocracy, all dressed in their most stunning finery. It was very festive. Tavi and Marco had been a part of this grand farewell party many times. They would dance, sing, wave and dream of the day that they would be sailing away instead of staying behind. "I can't believe that someday is today," said Tavi.

Dawn broke over the horizon. The buildings of Venice were black silhouettes against a pink sky. Nineteen galleys crowded the docks of *Molo di San Marco*. They rode low in the water, laden with European linen and wool destined for Persia. A non-stop parade of men carried even more cargo up their gangplanks. Hundreds of gaily-decorated gondolas darted like mosquitoes in and out between the huge galleys.

Mama hugged Tavi so tightly that he could barely breathe, but he let her. "I hope that we packed everything you will need," she said, as they watched his trunk being carried aboard.

"Your father's maps, a prayer book from your mother, a quill and ink, three blank journals and a book of poems from me," his *grand zio* said, patting Tavi on the head.

Mama added, "Your fork and knife, a pewter goblet, three dozen candles, a warm coat, a change of clothes, a rosary, a blanket and two pillows."

His seven brothers surrounded him, for once not teasing. "Tavi, we are counting on you to keep your eyes open for good opportunities, to make a profit for all of us," said Philipe, handing Tavi a heavy leather pouch.

Tavi peered inside and gasped, "This is so much money!" Sure enough, it was filled with silver coins.

"There are sixty-four *libra denariorum venetialium* there," Philipe told him. "You will get your inheritance in six months when you turn twelve, so eight of them are yours—an advance. Then, we each added eight coins to give you a good stake. Eight for eight! You know we invest in everything as a family!" The brothers all smiled and nodded. "Remember our talks these last days?" Philipe reminded Tavi. "I think you will do just fine, and the Polos will always be there for advice." Then, everyone began talking at once.

"Tie that pouch around your neck."

"And tuck it inside your shirt, under your belt."

"And don't mention it to anyone."

"Put it to good use."

"Be careful! Don't get hurt."

"Don't lose that money."

"Keep an account of how you spend it."

"Bring back something pretty."

"Send us a letter."

"Take my spinning top with you for luck."

His brothers and sisters-in-law, nieces and nephews swarmed around him, patting his back, hugging him and tousling his hair. Tavi let his family's love engulf him. He kissed everyone—some of them twice. He stuck the toy top in his tunic and nervously fiddled with the pouch of coins. Suddenly, he didn't want to leave them.

"Follow your nose, sweet one. Bring me stories about the food you eat and the people you see," Mama said softly. She managed a weak smile as she quickly wiped away a tear and kissed him on both cheeks. She held his face in her hands and looked him straight in the eye. "You are your father's son. I know you will spot many things that others don't notice. You will make us all proud."

"Write your stories down, so you remember everything," said his *grande zio* in a cheery voice. "We will want to hear details, details, details!"

"Tavi, come on or you'll miss the boat!" Marco called out above the crowd. He was already onboard.

"Here. For emergencies." Mama thrust a bulging, brown burlap sack into his hands. Tavi gave her one last kiss and hug and ran up the gangplank. He was the last one to board. A sailor pulled the plank up behind him, and the purser checked his name off the list. Suddenly, twenty-four trumpets blew, and forty-six oars swept through the water. They were off! There was no turning back now.

The galley swiftly pulled ahead. It threw him off balance a bit. Tavi held on to ropes and carefully made his way across to the stern. Then he climbed the stair to the very top of the poop deck where Marco was. Tavi heard a loud groan from the deck below and leaned out to see 138 men moving their long oars in unison through the water. He looked back as Mama quickly shrank into the distance, framed between the famous columns of Venice.

"S-ciàvo Mama!" He waved furiously. Shimmering in fading pastels, Venice grew smaller and smaller, the sounds of the trumpets diminished, and the golden domes of San Marco melted away. Then pouf! Tavi's home-town—the only place he had ever been in his eleven and one-half years, the city he knew like the back of his hand, the center of his universe—vanished. A pain stabbed his heart. "What have I done?" he asked.

Marco patted him on the back. "You have taken the first step on the adventure we have dreamed of all our lives! Remember our rule?" They chanted, "North, south, east, west, there's one direction we like best: Onward!" It made Tavi laugh and washed away all but a ghost of his heartache.

"I think I know what Mama means by bittersweet," he said. "I'm excited and sad at the same time."

"Come on," said Marco. "Let's go see what's ahead." They clambered to the very edge of the beak shaped prow. Its menacing dragonhead seemed ready to take on all comers. Their ship was in the lead, its pennants flying. The eighteen other galleys fanned out behind and to both sides of them, like a sailing arrowhead. To their left, the coast of Croatia was in the far distance. Dead ahead was nothing but the azure water of the Adriatic Sea. At the horizon, the blue sea blended imperceptibly into the blue sky. "We're not pretending now!" said Marco. His voice was swept away in the salty sea spray.

Suddenly the wind gusted, the sails billowed, and the convoy picked up speed. Their red and gold hulls cut through the choppy waves like a set of knives slicing through soft butter. "I'm ready for anything!" said Tavi, and he really meant it. "When do we get to Acre?"

"Well, if we average nine knots," Marco said as he counted on his fingers, "it will take us a little over a week, plus the stops we make, so about ten days."

"Nearly two weeks before I step foot on any land?" exclaimed Tavi. "Today is Thursday, August 8, 1275, so that means Sunday, August 18. I am going to write the days down and keep track."

"Do I get a prize if I'm right?" laughed Marco. "Don't worry, there will be plenty of excursions. We'll have to go ashore along the way and pick up goods in our colonies to sell later. We'll stop in Croatia, Negroponte and Cyprus to pick up olive oil, cheese, dried apricots, nuts and honey."

"Ooooh. I hope we get to eat some of those goodies. I mean goods!" Tavi's mouth watered just thinking about sweet, tender apricots. "Where do you think we will stop first? I can't wait to see the markets."

"You! Always with the food!" Marco shook his head. "Hey, what's in the bag?"

"A present from Mama. Let's see," said Tavi as he wrestled with the knot. "For emergencies she said."

"Food emergencies, that is," laughed Marco. The bag was stuffed with a dozen Fonero focaccia.

"I like the way she thinks," smiled Tavi.

EXPLORING THE GALLEY

Tavi reached in the sack and pulled out a crusty focaccia topped with roasted mushrooms, rosemary and garlic. He tore it down the middle and gave half to Marco. Then he stashed the rest of the bag in what he hoped was a dry place. The two of them happily munched as they set off to explore their new home from top to bottom. "I want to know this galley as well as I know Venice," exclaimed Tavi, "its every nook and cranny." Marco nodded and led the way up several sets of ladders to where the Captain was at the back of the ship.

"Sir," asked Marco. "Can you tell us about your galley?"

"Of course!" said the tall Captain as he looked up from his compass. He spread his strong arms wide in a sweeping gesture. "This whole area is called the *poop deck*. See, it is three stories tall. We are at the very top, where I pilot the ship," he explained. "It's called the *castle*. This is also where my cabin is. So it's like you are visiting my home up here." He then pointed to the floor below them. "That level is the *poop proper* where you and our other passengers will join me for meals. The lower level is the *pizolo* where your father and uncle, and other of my distinguished passengers, will bunk. Now go on. Explore. You boys have the run of my ship as long as you don't get in the way. And you have an open invitation to visit me in my castle anytime."

"Woo hoo!" Tavi yelped, as he and Marco scrambled down the ladders of the poop deck to the main deck. There in the center was a towering round post called the *mast*.

"This looks made for climbing," said Marco with a mischievous smile. "Bet I can beat you to the top!"

"Oh yeah?" said Tavi. Up they shot, picking their way through the rigging ropes above the billowing white sail to the very tiptop. They were both panting hard when they reached the tiny round *keba* platform and squeezed in. It was pretty near a tie.

"I won!" declared Marco. Tavi was about to argue, but he looked down, and the view stopped him short.

They were sixteen meters in the air! "The people on deck are so small, they look like ants," he exclaimed, "and I can see forever!" All around, there was nothing but blue in every direction. "We are flying!" yelled Tavi, spreading his arms to mimic the gulls that soared around him, trying to steal his focaccia.

"You boys get down here, before you kill yourselves!" shouted Niccolò.

"Yes sir," they said in unison. They shimmied down the mast and landed in a large open space on the main deck that everyone called *the marketplace*, because passengers met there to visit. Several men were gathered, talking, but the boys didn't stop to listen. Instead they climbed down through the large square hole in the deck to the *hold*. Marco had to duck his head to walk in the dark crowded space.

"Marco, is this really where people sleep?" asked Tavi. He eyed hundreds of hard wooden bunks stacked against both sides of the hold like beehives in a cave.

"Yes," said Marco. "The oarsmen, the sailors, even some of the passengers all sleep down here."

"I hope we don't have to," said Tavi. "It's so crowded. Look, there isn't enough space to even sit up. And you better hope no one snores."

They poked around and found lots more cargo stored in the hold. There was a carpenter's workshop, a couple of enclosed cabins and a locked closet, too. "Probably the armory," said Marco.

Tavi's eyes got as big as saucers. "I've never seen a hand cannon or a crossbow!"

"If we are lucky, you won't see these," said Marco, "because hopefully we won't run into any pirates. That's why we sail in a convoy. It's for protection. Lone ships are easy targets."

"Whew," said Tavi as they climbed out of the hold, back up to the main deck. "Too dark and stuffy down there for me! No windows! Hey, what's this?"

Lining the main deck against the high sides of the ship were casks, glass jars, ceramic jugs, trunks and all manner of cargo. It was stashed under and between the hard benches where officers slept. Above the benches, narrow catwalks ran from the very front to the very back of the ship down both of its sides.

Tavi and Marco hopped up onto a catwalk so they could see the oarsmen below. A cantilevered platform extended out about five feet along the full length of the ship. There was a matching one on the other side. They were each lined with twenty-three benches set at an angle to the outer edge where special notches were cut for the oars. Three men sat on every bench, and together each trio maneuvered one of the forty-six oars. The boys were transfixed as they watched the boatswain bang on a big board with a mallet as he paced. "It sounds like a wooden gong," said Marco. With each loud clunk, the rowers pulled back their huge oars in perfect harmony. "Smooth as Chinese silk," observed Marco appreciatively.

Suddenly, Tavi caught a whiff of something. "That is definitely the smell of onions frying. Someone is cooking, but where?" he asked. He ran down the catwalk back toward the castle, hunting for the source of the familiar aroma.

"Hey! Slow down!" yelled Marco, trailing behind for a change.

"Goats! Did you hear that bleating?" called Tavi over his shoulder. The catwalk ended at a fenced platform beside the poop deck. Sure enough, there was a pen with six goats, two sheep and eight pigs.

"What are they doing here?" asked Marco.

"Maybe waiting to visit this guy! I think I found the cook," shouted Tavi as he climbed on top of the goat pen to get a better look at the open-air kitchen above it.

He saw a large scary-looking fellow. A red handkerchief covered his thick mass of black curly hair, and a full beard nearly obscured his mouth. His sleeves were rolled up to the elbow revealing strong, tan forearms. He wore a big apron that may have actually been white at one time, but not anymore. The fire roared in the hearth behind him under a large, black bubbling cauldron. He chopped turnips, onions and carrots with a huge knife. Looking up, his blue eyes pierced right through the boys. "Anything I can do for you gents?"

chapter 5

LIFE ABOARD THE SHIP

Tavi woke on Friday just in time to see the rising sun paint the sky in a thousand shades of purple. It was magical. He paced up and down the port-side catwalk munching on bread and cheese. They were fully under sail with the oars up, so the only sound was a soft wind pushing them across the sea. Dolphins frolicked in the water, jumping over the wake of the galley like playful escorts. Their convoy had sailed all night, navigating along an ancient shipping lane known as the Spice Route. It was a quietly busy dawn. About 100 yards away, a line of galleys silently passed going the opposite direction. Tavi supposed that every ship was loaded with merchants returning to Venice with their exotic Eastern treasures. Suddenly, a wisp of homesickness swept over him. "I could go back so easily," he thought. But he quickly shook off the notion. "No! I am ready for adventure!" Marco walked up, full of energy. "I thought that we should use our time at sea to get ready for the rest of our journey," he said. "Let's study our geography, so we will know where we're going. And Latin, too, because *zio* Maffeo says it is the language of commerce."

"Great idea! And lets do counting drills, so that we can make a shrewd trade when the time comes!" added Tavi. They found a spot on the main deck at the corner of the marketplace. The boys sat there cross-legged all morning poring over maps, and they eavesdropped unnoticed on the adult conversations that buzzed around them.

Niccolò and Maffeo stopped by to check on them and nodded approvingly. "The more you know about where we are going, the more successful trader you will be," Niccolò told them. "Merchants have made their way across the world for centuries, buying and selling goods, spreading ideas and customs, even religion."

Maffeo chimed in, "They work like relay racers. Europeans come to Venice to buy goods from the East. To provide those products, Venetians sail to Alexandria, Constantinople or Acre. There, they negotiate with traders who come from China, Sumatra, India or Africa, either overland on the Silk Roads, or by sea along the Spice Route."

"It sounds like most traders just go back and forth between cities in the middle and never see where the goods actually come from or where they are finally used!" said Tavi. "Isn't that boring?"

"I guess not, because they make a good living at it," laughed Maffeo. "Many times they trade goods for goods. That's called bartering. In the most mountainous regions of the Silk Roads, cash is rarely spent. Every thing is barter."

"What am I going to do with all this money then?" asked Tavi, patting his side.

"I would convert it to something valuable for barter before we leave Acre. Something to trade along the way," advised Maffeo. "I can tell you, every man on this ship, from first mate to oarsman, has a stash of treasure. Everyone's a trader!"

"So, Papà," said Marco, "is the idea to trade for something compact and valuable, and then at the next stop, trade that for something else smaller and even more valuable?"

"Yes, son," replied Niccolò. "As you travel, you keep trading, one thing for another, each time at a profit. Spices like saffron, black pepper, cinnamon, cumin, nutmeg, ginger, cloves, and turmeric; fine cloths like silk, satin and woven rugs; musk, perfumes and medicines; jewels, like rubies, sapphires, pearls and emeralds; and other precious commodities—ivory, tortoise shell. If you are skilled, you'll be going home with a lot more than what can fit in that trunk you brought. And you will sell your goods at a handsome profit."

"We will have the best shop at the Rialto!" crowed Marco. "Stuffed with the treasures we find!"

Tavi's head swam with the possibilities. "I think it would be excellent if I could find something that no one has taken back before. I had better keep my eyes open. I need my own fork," he said, thinking of his father. The men nodded and agreed, "Yes. The Next Big Thing, also known as Tavi's Fork!" They all laughed.

The deck got hotter under the unrelenting noonday sun. People slowly disappeared. The officers and passengers re-assembled in the cooler poop deck for a big dinner. Afterward, they lounged under tarps strung up for shade. Some read. Others played cards or wrote in their journals. At sundown, they gathered again for a light supper. Tavi was spellbound by the conversation at mealtimes when fantastic stories unfolded. They were told with great relish and drama. It reminded him of a boisterous Fornero supper, except the reports were from all over the world, like their tellers, exotic and fascinating.

After supper, night fell like a black velvet curtain. The sky glittered with diamonds brighter than Tavi had ever seen. They mesmerized him. His neck hurt from looking up. "Look at that one!" he pointed out to Marco. "It is ten times brighter than the others." Just then a young man walked by and gestured to the sky.

"That one is the first star every evening at dusk and the last star remaining at dawn. But it ends up over there in the morning," said the *gallant* as he traced an arc in the sky from west to east. Gallants were the twelve most important seamen aboard, the ones who navigated the ship and furled the sails. This one spoke Venetian, but with a heavy Greek accent. "My ancestors thought that they were two different stars. They called the evening star *Hesperus*, grandfather of the *Hesperides* goddesses who guard the golden apples of eternal life. But now we call it *Aphrodite*, the goddess of love. We have stories about all the stars. If you draw an imaginary line from one to the others, you can see many things. We find gods, great heroes, even battles," the gallant went on. "See the outline of those stars over there? Can you make it out? It's a galley like ours!"

"Yes," said Marco. "I've heard the tale of that ship in the sky, but I have never seen it so clearly before.

Argo Navis. The ship of Jason and the Argonauts, sailing to fetch the Golden Fleece."

"I like the story of Jason. He was a hero who had many fine adventures on his quest. Will we fetch a Golden Fleece on our adventure?" joked Tavi.

"Maybe so," the gallant said good-naturedly as he walked away.

It had been a very long day, but the boys were still so excited, they stayed up quite late. The low murmuring conversations of fellow passengers enveloped them like a cozy blanket. They let their imaginations run rampant, making up their own adventures about the clusters of stars. "See those?" Tavi pointed. "Look, it's at least twenty stars encircling two bright ones in the middle—right there. There they are—all my brothers and their families, even my *grande zio*, with Mama and Papà in the middle. Everyone is watching over me."

"Ah yes, the famous Fornero Cluster!" said Marco with mock seriousness. "I know it well."

Gradually the other passengers disappeared leaving just the two of them. It was nearly midnight, and everyone else was safely tucked into their cabins or in the hold below. "I really don't want to go back down there tonight. Do you?" asked Tavi.

Marco shook his head no. "I found some hammocks. Let's string them up and sleep on the top deck," he suggested. So, that's what they did. The cool night breezes caressed them as they swayed gently with the waves, gazed at the stars and ate another one of Mama's focaccia. "Thank goodness your Mama sent these," Marco said. "The cook is nice, but his cooking . . . not so nice."

"Yes, I miss her so much," replied Tavi sleepily. "I need to make notes for her about all the things we've discovered in just two days. You're right about the food, though. I hope it gets better."

chapter 6

THE FOOD GETS BETTER

"It's a good thing the stories are great, because the meals are definitely not up to Fornero standard," Tavi complained to Marco after breakfast on Saturday. "Stew, salted meat, biscuits, there is nothing to bother mentioning to Mama! I've been trying to figure out what I can do about it."

"Why don't you start hanging around the kitchen so you can look for the right moment?" suggested Marco.

"Good idea!" Tavi agreed. He began paying daily visits to Cook. On Sunday, he couldn't think of anything to suggest. On Monday, when he realized that Cook was grating cheese and making pasta for losyns, he saw his opportunity. "Have you ever used cinnamon?"

"Boy, stick to your studies," Cook barked at him.

"My mama used to put it in her losyns. I still dream of it," Tavi replied with a note of homesickness. He felt a little guilty giving away his Mama's secret, but times were desperate.

Cook looked up. "Oh she did, did she?" he said. "I never heard of that. But if it will make you stop mooning around here, I'll toss some in."

The losyns was a big hit at dinner. When everyone praised the meal, Tavi was quick to credit Cook's ingenuity. The Captain knew better. He had sailed with Cook for years and doubted a miraculous transformation had occurred. Besides, he knew the Fornero reputation and figured that Tavi was involved somehow.

"I hear that your mother has a great nose," the Captain said. "Is that a family trait?"

"I wish it was. Though people say I favor her, I think they mean my looks," replied Tavi. "I did use to help her by finding ingredients." He was suddenly emboldened by an idea. "In fact, I've been meaning to ask if I could go with the shore party tomorrow, sir. To Negroponte? I would be happy to help look for provisions; maybe find something interesting? I would stay out of the way." Tavi tried to sound casual, off-handed.

"Great idea, son!" the Captain quickly agreed. Marco winked at Tavi from across the table. He grinned back and mouthed "yes!" The conversation then veered to the exchange rate, but Tavi could no longer concentrate on what anyone was saying. He was thinking about tomorrow's adventure.

Tuesday morning, Tavi was up well before dawn. He stood eagerly watching from high atop the Captain's castle as they sailed toward a large Aegean island off the coast of Greece. "You know it's a Venetian colony,"

said Marco, joining him.

"I know, but somehow I expect it won't be a thing like home," replied Tavi as they eased into the harbor.

There was a buzz of activity onboard as the sailors tossed out ropes to tie down the ship and prepared to go ashore. Most of them didn't get very far, only to the bottom of the gangplank where it was dropped on the dock. There they set up an impromptu bazaar and laid out their small bundles of treasures for sale to all who strolled the wharf. An air of festivity prevailed as crowds milled around to shop, but Tavi's group was on a mission, so they didn't pause. They walked down the gangplank and pushed through the throng into town.

Tavi's intuition was right. The whole feel of Negroponte was different from Venice. Venice and its canals were rendered in a hundred shades of subtle pastels. Negroponte was a vivid two-tone palette of white and sapphire blue. White-washed stucco buildings crowded onto steep streets that led up from the sparkling sea. The *agora*—that's what they called their market—was a maze of hundreds of colorful tarp-covered stalls. It hummed at a low roar with dozens of languages, reminding Tavi of the Rialto. What extraordinary things Tavi saw as he trailed Cook through the teaming bazaar. Tavi kept letting his nose distract him, and he would fall behind to poke into this and taste that, then run to catch up to his group. "Please stay with us!" called Cook.

Not one of them could resist lingering at one stall where long skewers of meat were grilling over hot coals. The smell was just too intoxicating. "These are *kalamaki*," said the vendor. "I marinate cubes of lamb meat all night in olive oil, lemons and oregano. Then I pierce them on this reed to cook." He handed their group each a skewer full of seared meat that was cradled in a soft, hot piece of flat bread. They eagerly ate it on the spot.

"Oh! It's so good! The bread is kind of like a focaccia, but thinner," exclaimed Tavi.

"We call it *pita*," chuckled the vendor. "To us it is everything: Food, utensil, even a plate!"

"That would be handy on a trip," said Cook.

"Let's buy some extra of these pitas," suggested Marco. "They feel like a little bit of home, don't they?" The boys each stashed half a dozen under their tunics and continued the shopping expedition.

"Mama would love to see this," Tavi said occasionally to grab Cook's attention as they scoured the market. Every time Tavi mentioned his famous mother, Cook would stop and reconsider things he had passed up. Tavi was nosing around a stall filled with produce—much of it familiar, when he saw something he didn't recognize. "What are these red and white roots that look like funny carrots?"

"Radishes," nodded the merchant offering one to Tavi as Marco and Cook briskly walked on. "Taste them.

Peppery. Sweet. You like?" One bite was like a small explosion in Tavi's mouth.

"It's splendid! Cook, please try this radish," he called out, stopping Cook in his tracks.

"My young friend is hard to ignore," winked Marco, "but you can trust his taste buds."

"OK," sighed Cook with an air of resignation. The Captain had told him to humor the boy.

While Cook and Marco tasted the radishes, a large green and purple thistle distracted Tavi. It was as big as a man's fist. "And this?" Tavi asked. "Why in the world would you eat this thorny thing?"

The merchant whipped out a large cleaver and whacked the thistle in half with one blow. That got everyone's attention. Then with a smaller knife, he carved out the spiky middle to reveal a delicate cream-colored interior. "Because they hold this treasure!" he smiled.

"Let's try! Why not? Please, Cook?" pleaded Tavi again.

Cook shrugged, "Why not, indeed?" and purchased a dozen.

The sailors who came along to carry their acquisitions staggered under the load. So far, besides the radishes and artichokes, they bought a small octopus, four dozen squid, jars of honey, ripe olives, a bin of grapes, a wheel of hard cheese, soft cheese in brine, onions, a braid of garlic and six drum fish.

They had just entered a stall filled with baskets of herbs, when Cook said, "Time to head back. The Captain will be expecting dinner. Besides, I don't see much use for these weeds." But it was clear he was enjoying himself.

Tavi ignored the comment. He moved through the stall, waving his hands in the air over each basket, wafting their perfumes toward his nose. He assembled a bouquet of oregano, thyme and basil. "Mama uses these all the time," he assured Cook. "Wait, I've never seen these before!" He held a up stalk of deep red berries and breathed in the aroma. "They smell like sunshine."

The turban-clad vendor did not speak Venetian or Italian, but he was eager to help. He repeated "sumac, soo-mack," and put a cluster in his mortar. He proceeded to pulverize it with his pestle, crushing it into a fine powder that glistened reddish-gold. The fragrance was even more powerful and lemony.

"But how do we use it?" asked Cook.

"Don't worry, I'll bet you will think of something!" said Tavi. "Let's just get it."

"We'll take six clusters," Cook relented, holding up six fingers. Marco laughed and shook his head. He knew his friend all too well. Tavi had a knack for beguiling people into doing things his way.

Trailed by a parade of sailors shouldering baskets and bundles, they boarded the galley like triumphant soldiers with their bounty. Tavi noticed the Captain watching them from his castle, and gave him a discreet wink. The Captain nodded conspiratorially. Tavi felt like a secret agent on a mission as he raced back to the kitchen platform. "May I experiment with the sumac?" he asked Cook.

"As long as you don't get in my way," said Cook as he worked quickly on dinner.

Tavi got busy with a mortar and pestle. First he ground the sumac berries into a fine powder. He mixed in grated hard cheese, olive oil, and smashed cloves of garlic. He kept smashing until it was all a smooth paste. He didn't really know why he thought of combining these things, but the aromas tickled his nose. "This would be so good spread on top of focaccia," he thought as he considered how his bag from Mama was slowly shrinking. "I wished I had paid closer attention to how it was made. I could kick myself. Wait!" He remembered his pita and took one out of his tunic. He spread it with the sumac paste. "Not bad at all," he decided as he cheerfully chewed.

"Can you use this on something?" he asked, offering Cook the mortar full of his new concoction.

Cook dipped his finger in to taste. "Maybe on the drum fish," he muttered to himself as he took the mortar. "Now get out of here! Young gentlemen don't belong in the kitchen. Go study!"

Let it be said that on that day, dinner was scrumptious. In the five days that followed, the meals just got better and better. It was as if someone had flipped a switch in Cook. That market visit inspired him to experiment with interesting ingredients at every meal.

At the supper table on Saturday night, they were feasting on artichokes and pine nuts when the Captain stood up. "Our friends are leaving us at Acre. Before they go, I want to extend my profuse gratitude. Thank you for your fine company. Most of all, thank you for the influence you have had on my dinner!" He patted his stomach and turned to Tavi. "Son, you have an indispensable talent! That nose of yours will make you many friends. You can count me as one of them." Everyone around the table applauded. It made Tavi blush.

"Thank you sir! Maybe I really do have my Mama's nose, magic and all."

The next morning, he made a note in his journal: "August 18, 1275. Last night the Captain that said I have an indispensable talent. Is this what I've been searching for? I wonder how I might make my fortune using my sense of smell? We arrive in Acre today. Hopefully I can figure it out there."

The sun was still low in the eastern sky when Tavi joined the Polos in the prow. "Look!" Niccolò scanned the horizon with his spyglass. In the far distance, Tavi could just make out massive grey stonewalls. The city of Acre rose 100 feet straight out of the water. His imagination reeled.

"Know what I think is behind those walls?" he asked Marco. "A whole world of new smells, new tastes and new adventures!"

"Then onward we go!" Marco replied.

to be continued

RECIPES FROM VENICE TO GREECE

flat bread & beyond

Pancakes 52

Basic Whole Wheat Flatbread 54

Easy Focaccia 54

Traditional Genovese Focaccia 58

Pita 60

Rustic Mushroom Tarts 62

pasta & rice

Basic Fresh Pasta Dough 66

Losyns (Cheese Lasagna) 70

Traditional Pesto 72

Za'atar Style Pesto 73

Pasta Primavera 74

Radishes & Greens with Pasta 76

Ravioli with Fresh Herbs 78

Artichokes & Orzo 80

Asparagus Risotto 82

proteins & veggies

Stuffed Eggs 86

Barley & Lentil Soup 88

Walnuts in Brussels 90

Roasted Vegetables with
   Gremolata 92

Spring Salad in Bloom 94

Homemade Yogurt 96

Greek Yogurt 97

Tzatziki 98

Kalamaki 100

Feta & Veggie Roll-ups 102

Fish Soup 104

desserts

Pears & Cinnamon 108

Saffron & Plum Cake 110

Fruit & Honey Bundles 112

Yiaourti Me Meli 114

flatbread & beyond

PANCAKES

Some people like to put the fruit on top of their pancakes instead of cooking it inside. That works too, just skip **#4** in **STEP TWO** and add your fruit with the nuts. Ever try a pancake sandwich with peanut butter and bananas in between two cakes? *Yum!*

MAKE SURE TO READ THE WHOLE RECIPE BEFORE YOU START!
Makes 24 pancakes (8-12 servings)

INGREDIENTS

- 2 cups whole wheat flour
- 1 teaspoon baking powder
- ½ teaspoon salt
- ½ teaspoon baking soda
- 2 eggs
- ½ cup low fat sour cream
- 2½ cups buttermilk
- 2 tablespoons honey
- 3 tablespoons + 1 teaspoon vegetable oil, divided *
- ½ teaspoon vanilla
- 1 cup fresh fruit, chopped into ½ inch cubes:
  bananas, strawberries, raspberries, apples,
  blueberries, pears, peaches, or whatever is in season
- ¼ cup chopped walnuts or pecans
- as needed: maple syrup, molasses, applesauce or honey for topping

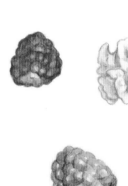

Preheat oven to 200°F.
Put a wire cooling rack on top of a cookie sheet and coat it lightly with a non-stick cooking spray. Set in oven.

STEP ONE: MIX IT UP

1. Measure and assemble all of your ingredients to create a *mise en place*.
2. Place flour, baking powder, salt, and baking soda in a bowl and stir with a whisk, until mixed well. Then make a well in the middle of the dry ingredients.
3. Place eggs in another bowl, whisk until lemon yellow.
4. Add sour cream to the eggs and whisk again to mix thoroughly. Get the lumps out.
5. Add buttermilk, honey, 3 tablespoons of oil and vanilla to the eggs and sour cream. Stir with a whisk until well combined.
6. Pour the buttermilk mixture into the well of flour mixture. Stir just enough to combine. Batter should be lumpy; don't stir too much.

Once upon a time

Did you know that pancakes were invented in ancient Rome? They were called Alita Dolcia, which is Latin for "another sweet." During Tavi's lifetime pancakes were perfected to the point that they were pretty much exactly what you eat today. Tavi loved pancakes for any meal, don't you?

STEP TWO: LAYER THE FLAVOR

1. Pour 1 teaspoon of oil into a cold non-stick skillet or griddle set over medium high heat.
2. When the oil starts to shimmer, wipe pan or griddle with a paper towel to evenly spread the oil across entire bottom of the pan, and turn heat to medium.
3. Use a ¼ cup dry measure to dip batter onto the hot pan, making 4 puddles.
4. Quickly drop a few pieces of fruit onto the top of each pancake batter puddle.
5. In about 30 seconds, bubbles will begin to pop-up in the batter, and the edges will begin to set. Flip cakes over to other side.
6. Brown the second side another 30 seconds to 1 minute, until cooked through. Be careful not to burn.
7. Slide cooked pancakes onto the wire rack you've set in the oven to keep warm while you cook the rest.
8. Wipe the pan between each batch of cakes with your oil soaked paper towel to leave a thin coating.

STEP THREE: SERVE

1. Remove pancakes to dinner plates, stacked 2 or 3 per person.
2. Sprinkle stacks with chopped nuts and garnish with fruit.
3. Serve with honey, molasses or real maple syrup.

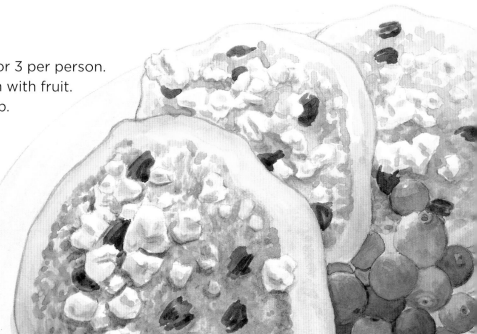

✳ When an ingredient says *divided* next to it, that means that a little bit will be used in one step of the recipe and the rest will be used in another part.

BASIC WHOLE WHEAT FLATBREAD

This basic whole wheat flatbread dough can be used for many recipes from pita to pizza.

MAKE SURE TO READ THE WHOLE RECIPE BEFORE YOU START!

INGREDIENTS

- 1½ cups whole wheat flour
- 2½ cups bread flour
- 2 teaspoons fine sea salt
- 1 package or 2¼ teaspoons active dry yeast
- 1¾–2 cups warm water (about 90°-105°F)
- 1½ tablespoons honey
- 2 tablespoons olive oil

STEP ONE: MIX

1. Measure and assemble all of your ingredients to create a *mise en place*.
2. Combine the flour, sea salt, and yeast in a large mixing bowl.
3. Stir together with a fork.
4. Stir honey and 2 tablespoons of olive oil into a 2-cup liquid measure with 1¾ cups of warm water.
5. Slowly pour the honey/oil/water mixture onto the flour in a circular motion, making a spiral.
6. Using a scraper, begin mixing the dry ingredients and liquids together in this way:
   - Hold the bowl with your left hand and the scraper in your right.
   - Slide the scraper along the edge of bowl, in a motion that lifts and turns the dry ingredients toward the middle to mix well with the wet ones.
   - Rotate the bowl clockwise, lifting and mixing dry with wet until there are no completely dry ingredients left.
   - Add up to another ¼ cup of water if the mixture is too dry.

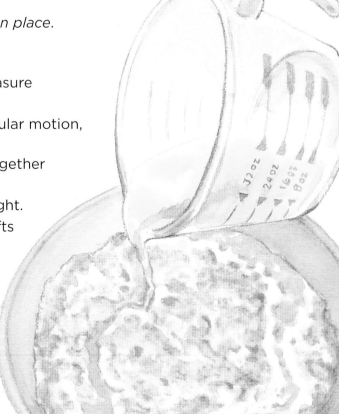

STEP TWO: KNEAD

You may want to wear latex gloves, but you don't have to. It is less messy to do this step in the same big mixing bowl.

1. Make a mound of the dough in the middle of the bowl.
2. Flatten the mound with your hands, then fold it in half toward you and push it down with your palms.
3. Turn the bowl 90° and fold dough in half again and push it down with your palms. Repeat this turning and flattening twelve times.
4. End with a nice smooth ball of dough.

What you do now depends on the recipe you want to make. Follow individual recipes for easy focaccia, pita, tarts, etc.

EASY FOCACCIA

This is not quite as rich as Traditional Genovese Focaccia (page 58), but it is easier and faster and very yummy.

MAKE SURE TO READ THE WHOLE RECIPE BEFORE YOU START!
Makes 24 servings

INGREDIENTS

- 1 recipe **BASIC WHOLE WHEAT FLATBREAD** (recipe on page 54)
- ⅝ cup olive oil, divided *
- 1 tablespoon water
- 1 tablespoon course sea salt
- 3-4 large sprigs fresh rosemary, leaves removed and chopped (discard the stems)
- optional: ¼ cup grated, low-sodium Parmesan cheese
  2 lemons, sliced crosswise very thinly

STEP ONE: THE RISING

1. Measure and assemble all of your ingredients to create a *mise en place*.
2. Prepare **BASIC WHOLE WHEAT FLATBREAD** recipe according to directions, but add an extra ¼ cup olive oil to the water before you mix it with the flour. You will get a much softer, stickier dough—that's perfect. Let the kneaded dough ball rise uncovered in its mixing bowl for 2-3 hours.
3. Select a large cookie sheet pan with 1-inch sides. Spread 2 tablespoons of the olive oil in a thick layer on the entire bottom and sides, using a paper towel or pastry brush.
4. Dump the risen dough into the middle of the oiled cookie sheet. With your hands, press the dough flat and evenly all the way to the sides.
5. Cover the sheet pan of dough with a clean dishtowel and let it rise for 3 hours. It will be puffy.

STEP TWO: PUTTING IT TOGETHER

1. Preheat oven to 450°F.
2. Make indentations all over the dough using your fingers. It should look like the moon surface, covered in small craters.
3. Combine ¼ cup of olive oil with the water, and whisk with a fork to emulsify.
4. Carefully drizzle the oil and water emulsion over the surface of the dough, especially filling the craters.
5. Sprinkle the rosemary and sea salt evenly over the top of dough.
6. If you are using Parmesan cheese, also sprinkle it evenly over the dough.
7. If you are using lemons, arrange the slices evenly all over the dough.

STEP THREE: BAKING THE FOCACCIA

1. Place sheet pan of dough into the pre-heated oven and bake for 15 minutes.
2. After 15 minutes, rotate the sheet pan, and continue baking until the lemons and the crust are golden brown, about 15 minutes more.
3. Remove pan from oven using oven mitts or potholders. Slide a spatula under the baked focaccia, carefully lifting it from the baking sheet, and transfer it to a wire rack to cool for at least 10 minutes before cutting and serving.
4. Place cooled focaccia on a flat cutting board. Using a pizza wheel, slice into 2-inch strips or fun shapes and enjoy!

✻ When an ingredient says *divided* next to it, that means that a little bit will be used in one step of the recipe and the rest will be used in another part.

get adventurous!

Create your own signature focaccia bread by experimenting with any combination of citrus, veggies and herbs. Don't be afraid to try other cheeses.

TRADITIONAL FOCACCIA GENOVESE

MAKE SURE TO READ THE WHOLE RECIPE BEFORE YOU START! You can either start authentic Focaccia Genovese early in the morning to have it finally coming out of the oven in time for dinner, or you can do Step One and Two in the evening, let the dough rise overnight and finish it the next day. (11 hours preparation time all together, but most of that is waiting for the dough to rise.)

As you can see, this recipe has a lot of salt in it. If you choose to reduce the salt, subtract it from **STEP TWO** and leave the coarse sea salt as a final topping.

Makes 24 servings

INGREDIENTS

- 3 tablespoons instant yeast
- 2½ cups water, divided
- 7¼ cups bread flour or 00 Italian pizza flour, divided *
- ⅝ cup extra virgin olive oil, divided
- 3 tablespoons coarse sea salt, divided
- 3-4 stalks fresh rosemary, leaves removed and chopped to equal ½ cup (stems discarded)

STEP ONE: MAKE A *POOLISH*

1. Collect and measure all of your ingredients to create a *mise en place*.
2. In a 4-cup measure or medium bowl, dissolve the yeast in ½ cup warm water (105°F). Add ¼ cup of flour and ¼ cup oil and mix thoroughly. Do not leave lumps.
3. Let the poolish rest in a warm place for 20 minutes.

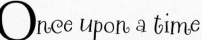

Once upon a time

Focaccia is thought to have originated in Greece, but very early in the 12th century it was adopted by Liguria where the port of Genoa, Italy is now located. It became the defining bread of Liguria. Focaccia Genovese is never thicker than one inch and traditionally topped with only rosemary and sea salt, but every family used their favorite ingredients as toppings—experiment!

STEP TWO: MAKE THE FOCACCIA DOUGH

1. In a very large bowl, mix the *poolish* with 5 cups of flour and the remaining 2 cups of water.
2. Combine thoroughly using your scraper in a circular motion around the bowl.
3. Mix remaining 2 cups flour and 2 tablespoons of salt together and then fold it into the dough. Blend well, using a circular lift and fold method with your scraper until no dry ingredients remain.
4. Scrape down sides of the bowl and then mound the dough in the middle. It will be runny.
5. Cover the bowl with a towel and let focaccia dough rise for 4 hours at a warm room temperature—about 78°F. It's OK to let the dough rise overnight.

STEP THREE: ANOTHER RISE

1. Using your fist, punch down the dough. It will be very soft and loose.
2. Select a large cookie sheet pan with 1-inch sides. Spread ⅛ cup of the olive oil in a thick layer on the entire bottom and sides, using a paper towel or pastry brush. Coat your hands with oil, too.
3. Dump the focaccia dough into the pan. Using your oily fingers, gently flatten and stretch the dough until it covers the entire bottom of the pan in one solid layer that is less than one inch thick.
4. Cover the pan lightly with a dishcloth, or another cookie sheet that is turned upside down, and set aside to rise for another 4-5 hours in a warm room (78°F).

STEP FOUR: FINISH IT

1. Preheat the oven to 425°F.
2. Add a tablespoon of water to remaining ¼ cup of oil and whisk with a fork to emulsify.
3. Oil your fingers. Pretend you are typing or playing the piano on the pan of dough to make holes all over it. The dough should still cover the entire surface of the pan, be less than one inch thick, and look like it's covered in craters like the moon.
4. Gently pour the oil and water emulsion onto the pitted dough to cover it evenly and fill the craters.
5. Sprinkle 1 tablespoon of coarse sea salt and the chopped rosemary evenly over the top.
6. Let the focaccia rest for 40 minutes in a warm room.
7. Bake for 25-40 minutes until light golden brown. Remove from oven using oven mitts or potholders.
8. Slide a spatula under the baked focaccia, carefully lifting it from the baking sheet. Transfer to a wire rack to cool for at least 10 minutes before cutting and serving.
9. Place cooled focaccia on a flat cutting board. Using a pizza wheel, slice into 2 inch strips or fun shapes.

❋ When an ingredient says *divided* next to it, that means that a little bit will be used in one step of the recipe and the rest will be used in another part.

PITA

Put a pizza stone in your oven. (If you don't have a pizza stone, turn a cookie sheet upside down and put it on the bottom rack of the oven.)

MAKE SURE TO READ THE WHOLE RECIPE BEFORE YOU START!
Makes 16 pitas about 6 inches in diameter

INGREDIENTS

- 1 recipe **BASIC WHOLE WHEAT FLATBREAD** (recipe on page 54)
- ⅛ cup olive oil
- extra flour for work surface

STEP ONE: RISING

1. Collect and measure all of your ingredients to create a *mise en place*.
2. Prepare **BASIC WHOLE WHEAT FLAT BREAD** recipe.
3. Lightly coat a medium mixing bowl with oil.
4. Place the kneaded ball of flat bread dough in the bowl.
5. Roll the ball of dough around in the bowl so that it has a light coating of oil on all sides.
6. Cover the bowl with plastic wrap or a damp kitchen towel and set aside to rise until it has doubled in size, approximately 90 minutes.

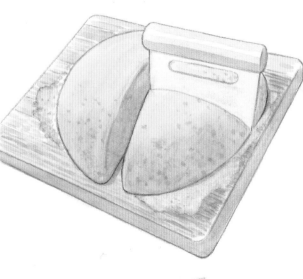

STEP TWO: DIVIDING

1. Pre-heat the oven to 400°F (with pizza stone or cookie sheet in it.)
2. When it has doubled in size, punch the dough down to release some of the trapped gases.
3. Using your scraper, cut the dough in half, cut each piece in half again, again and again—4 cuts in all—to end up with 16 small pieces. (If you want bigger pitas, divide the dough into fewer, larger portions.)
4. Roll each dough piece into a small (2-3 inch) ball and place on a sheet of parchment.
5. Cover the 16 small dough balls with a damp kitchen towel, and let them rest for 20 minutes.

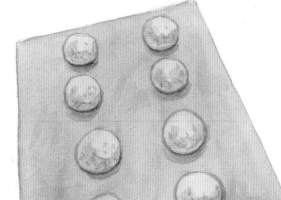

STEP THREE: ROLLING OUT

1. Spread a light coating of flour on your work surface, and lay out a dishtowel next to it.
2. Take one ball of dough, and roll it around in the flour to make sure all sides are covered.
3. Use a rolling pin or your hands to stretch and flatten the dough into a 6-inch circle that is between ⅛ and ¼ inch thick.
4. Dust both sides of the circle of dough with flour to lightly cover it completely.
5. Set the rolled-out, dusted pita circle aside on the dishtowel and cover with another towel while you finish making the rest of the pita circles.
6. Add a fresh dusting of flour to your work surface for and begin with a new ball of dough, repeating steps 1-5 above until you have 16 pita circles under the dishtowel.

STEP FOUR: COOKING

1. Place as many pitas as you can fit side by side without touching on the very hot baking surface in your oven (the stone or upside down baking sheet).
2. Bake each batch of pitas for 3 minutes until they start to puff up and turn a little brown. Remove pitas to a plate with a spatula. Stack them so that you flatten the puffing a bit, but don't smoosh them down hard.
3. Repeat baking batches until all pitas are cooked.

Be careful! The pitas will be full of hot steam. Best to let them cool before you try to open the pockets. Gently open up 3-4 inches of the edge and separate the walls of the pitas to reveal the pocket inside and then fill it with Kalamaki, or any fun combination of ingredients that you might like in a sandwich. Enjoy!

get adventurous!

Split the cooked and cooled pitas open to separate the sides completely. Then lay each side flat and cut like a pie into 8 triangles. Spread the triangles on a baking sheet and cook in a 200°F oven for 12 minutes. Viola! Baked Pita Chips!

RUSTIC MUSHROOM TARTS

MAKE SURE TO READ THE WHOLE RECIPE BEFORE YOU START!
Makes 12 servings as a side dish

INGREDIENTS

- ½ **BASIC WHOLE WHEAT FLATBREAD** (recipe on page 54); after 90-minute rise, divided into 12 balls
- 2 tablespoons olive oil
- 1 leek, thinly sliced or chopped fine, white part only
- 8 ounces fresh mushrooms—a selection of chanterelle, cremini, oyster, shitake, portabella, or just simple white button mushrooms roughly chopped. Use a damp paper towel to remove the soil rather than rinsing mushrooms.
- 2 tablespoons sherry vinegar
- 1 clove garlic, minced
- several sprigs of thyme, leaves removed to equal 1 tablespoon (stems discarded)
- ½ cup ricotta cheese
- ½ cup soft goat cheese
- salt and pepper to taste
- ½ cup Gruyere cheese, grated

Preheat oven to 400°F.

STEP ONE: MAKE THE FILLING

1. Collect and measure all of your ingredients to create a *mise en place*.
2. Heat oil in a medium sauté pan or skillet over medium low heat.
3. Add the leek and sauté while you stir with a wooden spoon until it is caramelized, about 20 minutes.
4. Add the garlic and cook another minute while stirring. Be careful; don't let it burn.
5. Add the mushrooms, turn heat to lowest setting, cover pan, and cook for 15 minutes.
6. Remove the cover and continue cooking until the mushrooms are browned and the liquid is nearly gone. Stir occasionally to keep from burning.
7. Add the vinegar, scraping the bottom of the pan to remove brown bits (this is called *deglazing*).
8. Remove the pan from heat and stir in the thyme leaves.
9. In a small bowl, combine the ricotta cheese and soft goat cheese and stir together with a fork, add salt and pepper to taste.

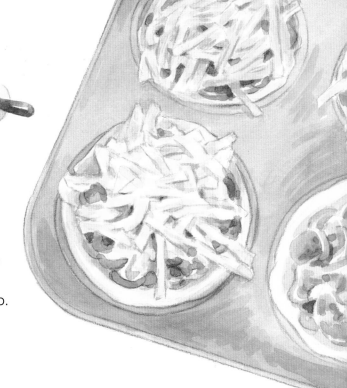

STEP TWO: ASSEMBLE THE TARTS

1. Lightly dust your work surface with flour.
2. Using a rolling pin, flatten each of the 12 dough balls into thin round discs about 5 inches in diameter and no more than ¼ inch thick.
3. Using your fingers or a paper towel, lightly coat the cups of a muffin tin with olive oil.
4. Gently lay the dough circles in the muffin tin, pressing the dough against the bottom and sides.
5. Spread 1 tablespoon of cheese mixture in the bottom of each cup.
6. Layer the mushroom mixture on top of the cheese.
7. Sprinkle the grated Gruyere cheese over top of the mushrooms.

STEP THREE: FINISH UP

1. Bake for about 25-30 minutes or until the crusts are nicely browned and the cheese is bubbling.
2. Remove from oven; allow to cool in the muffin tin on a rack for about 5 minutes.
3. To serve, slide a table knife around the inside of each muffin cup to loosen the tart, and gently lift it out.

tavi's tip

These tarts are still yummy even after they have cooled to room temperature, and you can eat them without a fork, so put one in your lunch! You can also make these tarts in advance and freeze them to use later. To use, remove from wrap, allow to defrost, place on a cookie sheet and reheat in a 350° F oven until the cheese bubbles (8-12 minutes.)

pasta & rice

BASIC FRESH PASTA DOUGH

MAKE SURE TO READ THE WHOLE RECIPE BEFORE YOU START!
The number of servings you get from this recipe depends on what you make with it.

INGREDIENTS

- 1 cup whole wheat flour
- 1⅔ cups all purpose flour
- 4 extra large eggs** (see notes on colored pasta)
- 1½ teaspoons extra-virgin olive oil
- optional for **CONFETTI PASTA**: ½ cup finely minced spinach or herbs

STEP ONE: MAKE THE DOUGH

Handmade Dough Directions:

1. Collect and measure all of your ingredients to create a *mise en place*.
2. In a large bowl, add the flour and make a well with your hands by swirling your index finger in small circles in the middle of the flour.
3. Break eggs into a small mixing bowl and make sure that there are no shells.
4. Beat the eggs until the yolks are broken and mixed in, and add the eggs into the center of the flour well.
5. Add the olive oil into the well on top of the eggs.
6. With a fork, gently and slowly mix the eggs in a circle. With each circle pull in some flour from the sides until it is fully incorporated and the dough comes together.
7. Lightly coat your hands in flour, and use them to flatten the dough, fold it in half and flatten again. This is called *kneading*.
8. Repeat the process of flattening and folding for about 2 to 3 minutes.

or instead you can use a food processor

Food Processor Directions:

1. Dump all of the ingredients into the bowl of a food processor and pulse until dough forms a rough ball, about 30 seconds. (If dough resembles small pebbles, add water, ½ teaspoon at a time; if dough sticks to side of the work bowl, add flour, 1 tablespoon at a time, and process until dough forms a rough ball.)

STEP TWO: REST AND DIVIDE

1. Cover dough ball with plastic wrap and set aside to allow it to rest for 30 minutes.
2. Divide dough into quarters and form into 4 balls.
3. Wrap 3 balls of dough in plastic that can be stored in the refrigerator for a week or in the freezer for a month. Keep one dough ball out to work with.
4. Flatten the ball with your hand.

Recipe continued on next page

tavi's tip

Do you know how to create brightly colored pasta? Red pasta can be made with beets and orange pasta with carrots. If you have herbs or spinach handy, you can make confetti pasta dough.

To make different colored pasta, use veggie purees. Instead of using 4 eggs in the recipe, use 1/2 cup puree, 2 whole eggs and 1 yolk. OR make confetti pasta by adding 1/2 cup finely minced spinach or herbs, and keep everything else the same.

BASIC FRESH PASTA DOUGH
(continued)

STEP THREE: MAKE THE NOODLES

By Hand:
1. Lightly flour a rolling pin and a work surface that is about 2 feet square.
2. Use the pin to roll out the dough into a thin sheet.
3. Flip the dough over and turn it 90 degrees, then roll it again to make it even thinner. Repeat the flipping, turning and rolling until your sheet of dough is thin enough to see your hand through.
   (You may have to add a bit more flour as you go to keep the pasta from sticking.)

or with a pasta machine

1. Feed the flattened dough ball through widest setting of a manual pasta machine and turn the crank to roll it into a sheet.
2. Fold both ends of the sheet of dough to the middle and press down to seal.
3. Feed dough, through the widest setting again.
4. Fold, seal, and roll again.
5. Without folding, run pasta through widest setting two more times. If the dough gets sticky, lightly dust with flour.
6. Continue to feed the dough sheet through machine; turning the knob to a narrower setting each time, until you use last setting on machine, and the outline of your hand is visible through the thin dough sheet.

STEP FOUR: CUT THE NOODLES

Use the cutting attachment on your pasta machine to make skinny or wide noodles.
   or
Use a pizza wheel or butter knife to cut long strips, triangles, rectangles or squares.
   or
Experiment with cookie cutters to make fun shapes like circles, stars, letters or numbers.
Drape the noodles over a spoon handle or lay on a cooling rack to dry slightly before cooking.

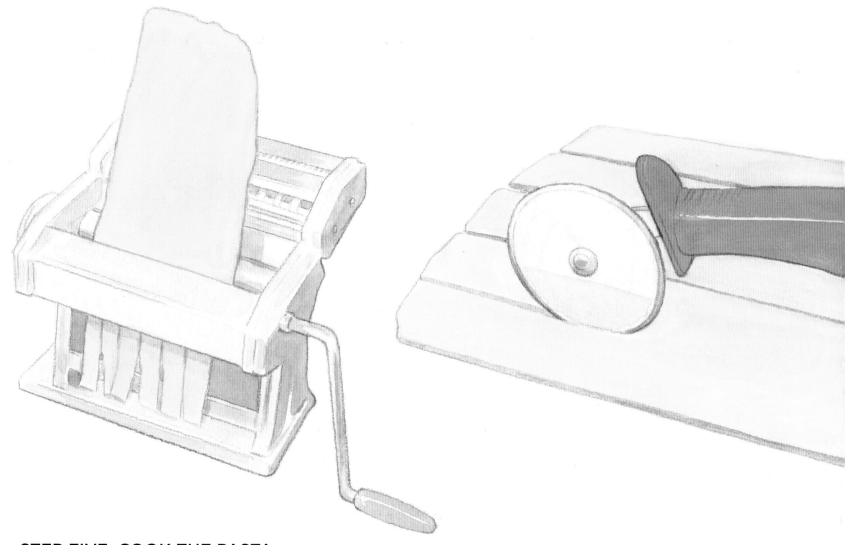

STEP FIVE: COOK THE PASTA

1. Drop the dried noodles into a pot of briskly boiling salted water and cook for 3 minutes. If pasta has been dried for longer than an hour, it may take up to 12 minutes to cook.
2. Drain the pasta into a colander, but hold back ¼ cup of the water in the pot.
3. Return pasta to the cooking pot and stir to keep it from sticking.
4. Add sauce to the hot pasta or use it in an assembled dish as directed.

LOSYNS

MAKE SURE TO READ THE WHOLE RECIPE BEFORE YOU START!
Makes 12 servings as a side dish or 8 servings as a main course

Once upon a time

Losyns was a medieval dish that used wide flat noodles, similar what we now call lasagna noodles. Layered with cheese, it was flavored with nutmeg and cinnamon. Here is how we think it was made.

INGREDIENTS

- 1 recipe **BASIC FRESH PASTA DOUGH** (recipe on page 66) or, 1 (16 ounce) box of commercial lasagna noodles
- 3 cups fresh ricotta cheese
- 2 eggs
- 1½ teaspoon cinnamon
- ⅓ teaspoon nutmeg
- 1½ teaspoon salt
- ¼ teaspoon fresh ground black pepper
- 8 cups fresh, rinsed and chopped spinach
- 4 cups shredded mozzarella
- ¾ cup grated Parmesan cheese
- ¼ cup fresh oregano leaves, coarsely chopped

Collect and measure all of your ingredients to create a *mise en place*.
Preheat oven to 350°F.
Lightly oil a 9×3×12-inch baking dish.

STEP ONE: THE NOODLES

If using freshly made pasta:
1. Follow directions for making fresh pasta.
2. Cut each sheet into 4×12 inch rectangles.
3. If you will make the dish immediately, then no need to boil the noodles, but if they are allowed to dry, follow instructions for dried noodles below.

or for dried noodles

1. Boil noodles according to package directions.
2. Drain noodles in a colander, reserving ¼ cup water in the pan, and return noodles to pot.

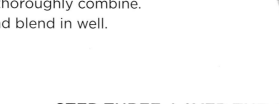

STEP TWO: MIX IT UP

1. Place the ricotta, eggs, cinnamon, nutmeg salt and pepper in a mixing bowl. Stir to thoroughly combine.
2. Add chopped spinach and blend in well.

STEP THREE: LAYER THE FLAVOR

1. Spread about ½ of the ricotta/spinach mixture to cover the bottom of the oiled baking dish.
2. Lay lasagna noodles, slightly overlapping each other, to completely cover the ricotta/spinach.
3. Cover the noodles with ½ of the mozzarella.
4. Cover the mozzarella layer with ½ of the Parmesan.
5. Repeat the layering process with the remaining ½ of your ingredients.
6. Sprinkle the top with the chopped oregano.
7. Place dish in oven. Bake for 35-40 minutes or until the cheese is bubbly and beginning to brown.

STEP FOUR: SERVE IT UP

Remove pan and allow it to cool for 5 minutes.
Cut Losyns into squares to serve.

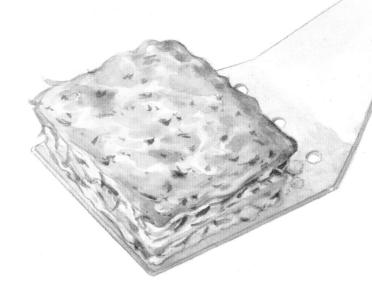

TRADITIONAL PESTO

MAKE SURE TO READ THE WHOLE RECIPE BEFORE YOU START!
Makes 1½ cups

INGREDIENTS

- 1 large garlic clove, peeled
- ¼ cup pine nuts
- ⅓ cup grated Parmigiano-Reggiano cheese
- 1 teaspoon sea salt
- ¼ teaspoon freshly ground black pepper
- 1½ cup loosely-packed fresh basil leaves
- ⅓ cup olive oil

LAYER THE FLAVOR

1. Collect and measure all of your ingredients to create a *mise en place*.
2. With the help of an adult, set up your food processor.
3. With the processor running, add the garlic clove and let it chop for 30 seconds.
4. Stop the motor and add the nuts, cheese, salt, pepper, and basil.
5. Process continuously until everything is finely chopped.
6. With the motor running pour in the oil in a very slow, steady stream.
7. Blend until mixed well, but not smooth.
8. Taste the pesto before serving, so you can adjust the flavors if you need to.

tavi's tip

Pesto is good on so many things: stir it into hot pasta, add to vinegar and oil salad dressing, use as a topping for baked fish or chicken, or even as a grilling sauce.

get adventurous!

You can change this basic pesto recipe a thousand ways. The only limitation is your imagination. Just use green herbs or leafy green veggies in place of the basil and any kind of nut in place of the pine nuts. Use almonds, pistachios, pecans, or even walnuts to make it different. Instead of basil, you could use cilantro or even arugula.

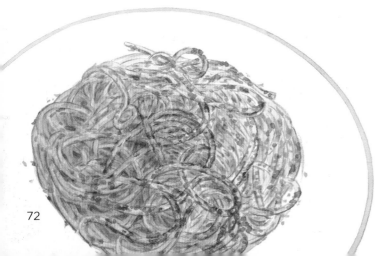

ZA'ATAR STYLE PESTO

Use this pesto in the same way you use traditional pesto—on pasta, in sauces and dressing, on grilled and baked meat. It tastes like sunshine with a uniquely Mediterranean flavor.

MAKE SURE TO READ THE WHOLE RECIPE BEFORE YOU START!
Makes 1½ cups

INGREDIENTS

- 4 cloves garlic, peeled
- ⅓ cup toasted sesame seeds
- 3 tablespoons dried ground sumac
- ½ cup Parmesan cheese, grated
- 1 teaspoon salt
- ½ teaspoon freshly ground black pepper
- 2 tablespoons fresh lemon thyme leaves
- ¼ cup fresh Mediterranean thyme leaves
- ¼ cup fresh chopped oregano leaves
- ¼ cup fresh chopped marjoram leaves
- 2 teaspoons honey
- 2 tablespoons tahini
- ⅓ cup olive oil

LAYER THE FLAVOR

1. Collect and measure all of your ingredients to create a *mise en place*.
2. With the help of an adult, set up a food processor.
3. With the processor running, add the garlic cloves and let them chop for 30 seconds.
4. Stop the motor and add the sesame seeds, sumac, cheese, salt, pepper, thymes, oregano, marjoram, honey and tahini.
5. Process about 1 minute, until everything is finely chopped.
6. With the motor running pour in the oil in a very slow, steady stream.
7. Blend until mixed well, but not smooth.

Once upon a time

Za'atar is used a lot like pesto, and we found it throughout Persia and the Middle East. Every family has its own recipe.

get adventurous!

Did you know that you can harvest and dry your own sumac? Staghorn Sumac grows in the woods of New England and blooms through August and September, putting out dense clusters of red berries, which can be harvested and dried.

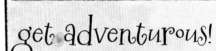

PASTA PRIMAVERA

MAKE SURE TO READ THE WHOLE RECIPE BEFORE YOU START!
Serves 8 as an entrée or main course

INGREDIENTS

- 1 recipe **BASIC FRESH PASTA DOUGH** (recipe on page 66), cut into
  ¼ inch wide noodles, cooked according to recipe or
  1 package (16 ounce) fettuccini-style dried noodles, cooked according to package directions
- ¼ cup olive oil, divided
- 2 carrots, minced
- 2 ribs celery, minced
- 1 small red onion, minced
- ¼ teaspoon salt
- 2 cloves garlic, minced
- 5 stalks flat-leafed Italian parsley, stems removed and minced
- 1 green onion, sliced thin
- 1 red bell pepper, julienned
- ½ bunch asparagus, tough stalks removed and tops cut into
  1 inch pieces, about 1½ cups
- 1 cup broccoli flowers, steamed for 3-4 minutes until bright green
- ½ cup peas (fresh or frozen)
- 2 ounces fresh spinach leaves, torn into bite-sized pieces
- 4-6 basil leaves, *chiffonade*
- ⅛ cup freshly grated Parmesan cheese

STEP ONE: MAKE A *SOFRITO*

1. Collect and measure all of your ingredients to create a *mise en place*.
2. Heat a large sauté pan to medium high heat and add ½ the olive oil; let heat up for 1-2 minutes.
3. Add minced carrots to the pan and sauté for 2 minutes.
4. Add minced celery and continue cooking 2 minutes.
5. Stir in the minced onion and cook until it starts to seem clear (about 5 minutes).
6. Add salt.
7. Add the minced garlic and continue cooking for about 2 minutes, or until it releases its wonderful *aroma* (smell).
8. Stir in the minced parsley.

You have just created an Italian-style sofrito, which if you stopped now, could be used as a great flavor base for soups, stews, and sauces.

STEP TWO: LAYER THE FLAVOR

1. Gently add the green onion, bell pepper, asparagus, and broccoli and cook for 3-4 minutes until all the veggies turn even brighter.
2. Stir in the fresh or frozen peas and spinach and remove pan from heat.
3. Add the pasta and the rest of the olive oil, and toss to coat.

STEP THREE: SERVE IT UP

1. Divide into shallow soup bowls.
2. Garnish with basil leaves, grated Parmesan cheese and a sprinkling of cracked pepper.
3. Serve immediately.

Once upon a time

Primavera means "the first green" in Italian. This dish was first created to celebrate young spring vegetables, but you can mix and match the veggies to make it with the best that any season has to offer. Here we make it with a little bit of everything.

RADISHES & GREENS WITH PASTA

MAKE SURE TO READ THE WHOLE RECIPE BEFORE YOU START!
Serves 6 as an entrée or main course

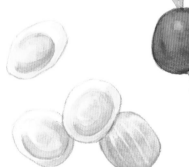

INGREDIENTS

- 2 tablespoons olive oil
- 2 cloves garlic, minced
- 1 medium onion, chopped
- 2 bunches fresh radishes with the leaves on, (preferably the small red and white ones, but any will do)
- 1 (12-ounce) package small, round, dried pasta such as orecchiette or shells
- ¼ cup cooking water left over from cooking pasta
- ⅓ cup freshly grated Parmesan or Romano cheese
- salt and pepper to taste

STEP ONE: PREPARE

1. Collect and measure all of your ingredients to create a *mise en place*.
2. Pinch the stems and leaves from the radishes.
3. Remove stems, and put leaves in a large bowl of cold water. Swish them around in the water to wash making sure to remove all traces of sand.
4. Lift from water and blot with paper towels or spin dry in a salad spinner.
5. Chop leaves coarsely.
6. Wash the radish bulbs well and slice thinly crosswise. Set aside.
7. Fill a large stockpot with water and set over high heat.

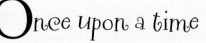

O*nce upon a time*

Who ever heard of radishes and pasta? Where have you been? This is how they did things in the 13th century.

STEP TWO: LAYER THE FLAVOR

1. Warm oil over medium heat in a large skillet that has a lid to fit it.
2. Add onion in one layer, cover the skillet and cook 5 minutes or until onion softens.
3. Remove lid, turn the heat to medium high and cook stirring constantly until onions begin to caramelize.
4. Add minced garlic and cook 1 more minute, or until you can smell it, stirring constantly to keep from burning or sticking.
5. Add radish slices and continue cooking until they also begin to brown just a little.
6. Add greens, stir to mix. Cover the skillet, reduce heat to medium low and cook for 5 to 7 minutes or until greens wilt and radishes look almost translucent. Remove from heat.
7. Season with salt and pepper to taste.

STEP THREE: FINISH THE DISH

1. When the stockpot of water comes to a boil, add pasta and cook for 12 minutes.
2. Drain the pasta in a colander set over the sink, reserving ¼ cup of the cooking liquid.
3. Add drained pasta to skillet of radishes and toss. Add cooking liquid from pasta pan and stir.
4. Stir in the Parmesan or Romano cheese.
5. Taste and adjust seasoning if needed.

Serve in shallow bowls, garnished with a pinch of Parmesan cheese and sprinkling of cracked black pepper.

RAVIOLI WITH FRESH HERBS

Ravioli are fun to make!

MAKE SURE TO READ THE WHOLE RECIPE BEFORE YOU START!
Serves 4-6 as an entrée or main course

INGREDIENTS

- 1 recipe fresh **CONFETTI PASTA** (recipe on page 66) made with minced spinach, prepared to the point of rolled flat sheets, cut to 6 matching rectangles, each approximately 15 inches long and 5 inches wide
- 1 cup fresh ricotta
- ½ cup minced fresh herbs—use a combination of what's in the your seasonal garden. Basil, oregano, marjoram, thyme, borage and sage were all herbs used in 13th century Venice
- ¼ cup toasted walnuts, finely chopped
- ⅛ teaspoon nutmeg, grated or powdered
- 1 cup grated Parmesan cheese, divided *
- 1 egg
- ¼ teaspoon salt
- squeeze fresh lemon juice (about ½ teaspoon)
- fresh ground pepper
- flour for work surface
- ½ cup prepared **TRADITIONAL PESTO** (recipe on page 68)

tavi's tip
You can also stir fresh veggies into your hot ravioli, just like you would with plain pasta. Try raw, fresh baby peas or spinach.

STEP ONE: THE FILLING

1. Collect and measure all of your ingredients to create a *mise en place*.
2. Combine ricotta with herbs, walnuts, nutmeg and ½ cup grated Parmesan, stir with a fork to mix well.
3. Add the egg, salt and fresh lemon juice, blend completely, set aside.

* When an ingredient says *divided* next to it, that means that a little bit will be used in one step of the recipe and the rest will be used in another part.

STEP TWO: LAYER THE FLAVOR

1. Spread a light dusting of flour on your work surface.
2. Lay one sheet of pasta down lengthwise in front of you on the counter.
3. Using a pizza cutter or table knife, cut pasta into rectangles that measure about 2½ inches by 5 inches.
4. Lay a little pasta rectangle on your work surface with the 5-inch edge toward you; put a teaspoon of filling in the middle.
5. Fold the right side across on top of the filling to completely cover it, but leave a ½ inch "flap" of uncovered pasta on the left.
6. Using a pastry brush, paint a little water along the edge of the ½ inch flap on the left.
7. Fold the left side over the top and press gently to make a seal. You are closing up your ravioli like an envelope
8. Press down all around the edges. Now the ravioli is sealed tight.
9. Repeat with the remaining rectangles of pasta and filling.
10. Lay the individual ravioli on a cooling rack until you are ready to cook them all.

STEP THREE: FINISH THE DISH

1. Fill a large stockpot with water and add salt, set pot over high heat and bring to a boil.
2. When the water starts to boil, carefully lower half of the individual ravioli into the water using a long-handled slotted spoon or a sieve.
3. Boil for 8 minutes, remove with a slotted spoon into a warmed shallow bowl, set aside.
4. Cook the remaining ravioli in the same way.

STEP FOUR: SERVE IT UP

1. For each serving, put 6-8 warm ravioli into a shallow soup bowl
2. Top with each serving with a dollop of pesto (about 1 tablespoon) sprinkle on 1 tablespoon grated Parmesan and cracked pepper to taste.

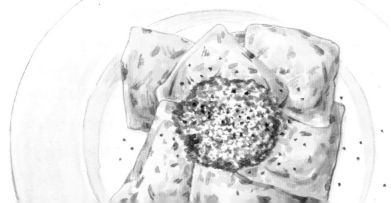

ARTICHOKES & ORZO

MAKE SURE TO READ THE WHOLE RECIPE BEFORE YOU START!
Serves 4-6 as an entrée or main course, or 8-10 as a side dish

INGREDIENTS

- 1½ cups dried orzo pasta (10 ounces)
- ½ heaping cup of nuts—raw walnuts, almonds or pine nuts
- 1 (14-ounce) can whole artichoke hearts in water, or
  1 (16 ounce) package frozen artichoke hearts, defrosted
- 4 tablespoons extra-virgin olive oil, divided ✳
- 2 cloves of garlic, minced
- 2 tablespoons red-wine vinegar
- ½ cup fresh parsley, finely chopped, plus 6 sprigs for garnish
- 1 teaspoon finely grated fresh lemon zest
- sea salt to taste
- fresh ground black pepper to taste
- grated Parmesan cheese

STEP ONE: BUILD THE DISH

1. Collect and measure all of your ingredients to create a *mise en place*.
2. Bring a 4- to 5-quart pot of water to a boil, add orzo, return to boil, reduce heat to simmer and cook for 8-12 minutes until just tender.
3. Pour orzo from pot through a strainer or sieve, but hold back ⅛ cup of water in the pot.
4. Return drained orzo to pot with liquid, add 1 tablespoon of olive oil, and stir to coat.
5. Add nuts to a dry small skillet set over moderate heat, and cook stirring constantly until they release their aroma and smell like really yummy nuts. When they just begin to toast, remove from heat, about 2 minutes.
6. Cool the nuts for 1-2 minutes, then chop coarsely.
7. Empty artichoke hearts into a large strainer or colander and run water over them to rinse well. You don't want any of that canned flavor left.
8. Pull the leaves off the artichoke hearts, and put in a colander; cut the hearts into quarters add to the colander, and set everything aside to drain well.

✳   When an ingredient says *divided* next to it, that means that a little bit will be used in one step of the recipe and the rest will be used in another part.

STEP TWO: LAYER THE FLAVOR

1. Heat 3 tablespoons of oil in a sauté pan and add garlic. Cook for 1 minute on medium-low until the garlic softens and releases its distinctive aroma.
2. Add artichoke hearts and leaves, and stir really well to combine, so that you don't leave any garlic stuck to the bottom of the pan. Cook until everything begins to brown.
3. Remove pan from heat and immediately pour in vinegar. Working quickly with a spatula, scrape the bottom of the pan clean, and mix the brown bits into the artichokes. This is called *deglazing*. The little bits give great flavor, so don't miss a single one!
4. Add in parsley, lemon zest and toasted nuts. Stir to mix evenly.
5. Spoon orzo into cooked artichoke mixture and carefully stir to distribute everything evenly.

STEP THREE: SERVE IT UP

1. Taste your dish and add salt and pepper to your liking.
2. Serve on individual plates garnished with a sprig of parsley, a pinch of grated Parmesan cheese and a few sprinkles of lemon zest.
3. Offer with freshly cracked pepper, accompanied by focaccia bread and a fresh green salad.

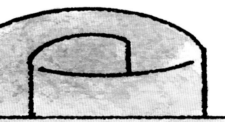

get adventurous!

This recipe can easily be made with fresh artichokes when they are in season and inexpensive.

1. Steam 6-8 fresh artichokes in a large stockpot of boiling water for about 45 minutes until they are tender.
2. Drain the water and let the artichokes cool completely. (Steps 1 and 2 can be done the day before).
3. Remove all the outer leaves and the "choke" itself. Only the hearts are used in this dish, save the leaves to eat as a snack. Discard the fuzzy inner choke. *The fun part of this is that you can nibble on the leaves as you remove them. Simply turn upside down and pull against your bottom teeth to scrape off the little bit of tender heart that is there. You won't be able to use any of these fresh leaves in your orzo recipe—they are too tough. So, snack away.*
4. Cut the hearts into quarters, then cut each quarter into 4 equal pieces and sauté with the garlic as described above in **STEP TWO**, **#2**, but remember—just use the hearts, not the leaves!

ASPARAGUS RISOTTO

MAKE SURE TO READ THE WHOLE RECIPE BEFORE YOU START!
Serves 4 as an entrée or main dish, or 8 as a side dish

INGREDIENTS

- 3 tablespoons olive oil
- 6 ounces fresh mushrooms, coarsely chopped—these can be a mixture of different kinds
- 8 ounces fresh asparagus, tough ends removed and stems cut into 1-inch pieces
- 1 cup finely chopped onion (it can be red, yellow or white)
- 2 cups Arborio rice (or you can use any short or medium grain rice from the store)
- 1 teaspoon salt
- 7 cups low sodium chicken, beef or vegetable broth at room temperature, divided
- 2 ounces grated Parmesan cheese, approximately ½ cup
- ½ teaspoon grated lemon zest
- ½ teaspoon grated nutmeg
- sea salt and freshly ground black pepper to taste

STEP ONE: BUILD THE DISH

1. Collect and measure all of your ingredients to create a *mise en place*.
2. In a large skillet set over medium high heat, warm 2 tablespoon of olive oil until it shimmers
3. Add mushrooms and asparagus, and sauté until the asparagus turns bright green.
   Stir to keep anything from sticking. Remove with a slotted spoon and set aside
4. Add another tablespoon of oil and the chopped onions to the pan.
5. Cook over medium heat, stirring occasionally, until the onions are almost see-through.
6. Add rice, salt and 3 cups of broth. Stir to combine.
7. Cook over low heat until the liquid evaporates.

STEP TWO: LAYER THE FLAVOR

1. Add 1 cup more broth to cover the rice.
2. Cook, stirring constantly until liquid is almost all soaked up.
3. Add another cup of broth to cover again. Continue cooking and stirring until the liquid is almost all soaked up again.
4. Repeat until you have used all the broth. This should take about 40 minutes in all from the first time you add the rice. That's a lot of stirring, but it's worth it!
5. Taste the risotto. The rice should be tender, and very creamy—not dry.
6. Gently stir in the mushrooms and asparagus.

STEP THREE: SERVE IT UP

1. Remove the pan from heat and stir in the Parmesan, lemon zest and nutmeg.
2. Taste your creation and season with salt and freshly ground pepper to your taste.
3. Serve in big shallow bowls with extra Parmesan cheese to pass.

tavi's tip

Experiment with different vegetable combinations in your risotto. Fresh or frozen peas and chopped carrots, tomatoes and basil, or broccoli—these are always good. And it can be fun to stir in a handful of fresh spinach at the very end, before you add the cheese. If you want, you can add a little spicy meat for flavor, like 2 ounces of diced ham or Italian sausage. If you use meat, add it to the onions when you sauté them.

get adventurous!

If you have the time, or want to take your skills to the next level, try this extra step to create a complex layering of flavors.

BEFORE STEP ONE: AN EXTRA STEP

1. Slice the asparagus stalks into one-inch pieces, make a pile of just the very tips and another pile of the stalks.
2. Put ½ of the stalks into a blender with 1 cup of broth. Purée and set aside.

STEP ONE: BUILD THE DISH (WITH A TWIST)

Follow directions through number 5. Instead of adding the rice and 3 cups of broth, add the rice, puréed asparagus and 2 cups of broth.

Finish with **STEPS TWO** and **THREE**

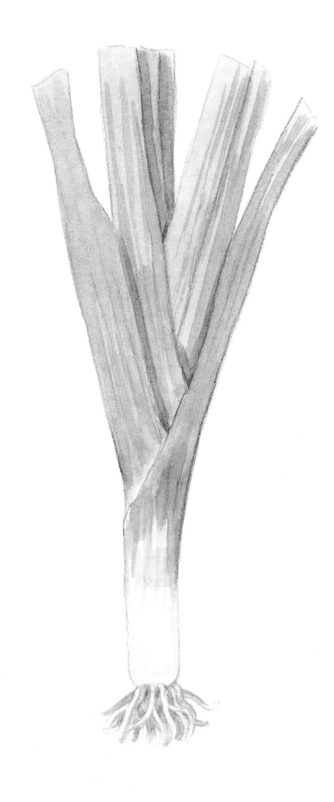

proteins & veggies

STUFFED EGGS

MAKE SURE TO READ THE WHOLE RECIPE BEFORE YOU START!
Serves 6-12 as a snack

INGREDIENTS

- 6 eggs, hard-boiled and carefully peeled
- 2 tablespoons fresh parsley, minced
- 2 tablespoons plain, low fat yogurt
- a pinch each of salt and pepper

To make them Savory and add

- 1 tablespoon mustard
- 1 teaspoon each: minced fresh basil, thyme and oregano
- ⅛ teaspoon paprika for dusting

or

To make them Sweet and add

- ⅛ teaspoon each ground ginger, cinnamon, and nutmeg
- 1 tablespoon honey
- ⅛ teaspoon extra cinnamon for dusting

STEP ONE: THE BASICS

1. Slice each egg in half lengthwise and carefully remove the yolk.
2. Collect yolks in a bowl
3. Arrange the whites cut side up on a plate
4. Mash the yolks together.
5. Add freshly chopped parsley and yogurt to the mashed yolks.

STEP TWO: LAYER THE FLAVOR

Make them Savory:

1. Add mustard, basil, thyme and oregano to the yolk mixture.
2. Thoroughly blend everything to make a smooth paste.
3. Carefully spoon yolk mixture back into the halves of whites.
4. Arrange on a platter and sprinkle with paprika.

or

Make them Sweet:

1. Add ginger, cinnamon and nutmeg and honey to the mashed yolk mixture.
2. Thoroughly blend everything to make a smooth paste.
3. Carefully spoon yolk mixture back into the halves of whites.
4. Arrange on a platter and sprinkle with cinnamon.

tavi's note

The egg halves will sit nicely on a plate if you first build a nest for them with leaves of lettuce. You can shred iceberg lettuce, or use the individual leaves of delicate Boston lettuce to make cups.

get adventurous!

Experiment with different ingredients and combinations added to the egg yolks, like curry, diced red bell peppers, onions, sun-dried tomatoes, celery, sweet pickles, capers or olives, cracked coriander or minced cilantro or basil, horseradish, salsa, pesto—almost anything can work.

BARLEY & LENTIL SOUP

MAKE SURE TO READ THE WHOLE RECIPE BEFORE YOU START!
Serves 10-12 as an entrée or main dish

INGREDIENTS

- 1 pound spicy Italian-style turkey sausage
- 2 cups water
- 2 tablespoons vegetable oil
- 1½ cups chopped onions
- 1½ cups chopped carrots
- 2 large parsnips, peeled and chopped (about 1¾ cups)
- 2 large celery stalks, chopped (about 1 cup)
- 4 large garlic cloves, minced
- 1 anchovy filet, mashed into a paste
- 10 cups low-salt vegetable broth
- 1 cup pearl barley
- 2 cups dried lentils, rinsed
- 4 cups coarsely chopped Swiss chard, kale or spinach (packed)
- salt and pepper
- 2 tablespoons chopped fresh oregano

STEP ONE: LAYER THE FLAVOR

1. Collect and measure all of your ingredients to create a *mise en place*.
2. Heat a heavy, large soup pot over medium-high heat.
3. Add sausage and the water; cook until water evaporates and sausage begins to brown.
4. Remove sausage and set aside to cool.
5. Add oil, onions, carrots, parsnips and celery to pot; sauté, stirring frequently until onions are golden brown, about 10 minutes.
6. Stir in garlic and cook for 1 minute.
7. Mix in mashed anchovy; stir to blend well.

STEP TWO: MAKE IT SOUP

1. Add 10 cups broth and the barley; bring to boil.
2. Reduce heat; partially cover and simmer 25 minutes.
3. Stir in lentils; cover and simmer until barley and lentils are both tender, about 30 more minutes.
4. Slice the cooled Italian sausage into 1-inch pieces
5. Add chard (or other greens) and sliced Italian sausage to soup; cover and simmer until chard is tender, about 5 minutes.

STEP THREE: SERVE IT UP

1. Stir in oregano. Season with salt and pepper to taste.
2. Serve in deep soup bowls, garnished with Parmesan cheese.
3. Store leftovers in the refrigerator to enjoy later. The flavors just get better and better over time (up to a week).

tavi's tip

This can be made without the sausage, just sauté veggies in 2 tablespoons of olive oil instead of sausage drippings

WALNUTS IN BRUSSELS

MAKE SURE TO READ THE WHOLE RECIPE BEFORE YOU START!
Serves 4 as a side dish

INGREDIENTS

- 16 fresh Brussels sprouts, washed, discolored outer leaves removed and stem cut off
- ¼ cup walnut oil
- 1 tablespoon honey
- 1 tablespoon balsamic vinegar
- ½ cup walnuts, coarsely chopped
- salt and pepper to taste

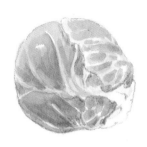

STEP ONE: PREPARE THE SPROUTS

1. Collect and measure all of your ingredients to create a *mise en place*.
2. Cut each sprout in half lengthwise and then in half again to make little wedges.
3. Place a veggie steamer into the bottom of a saucepot that has a lid, and add water to just below the steamer.
4. Bring water to a boil over high heat.
5. When you can see that the water is bubbling, place the 16 sprouts into the steamer and put on the lid.
6. Steam for 8 minutes or until the sprouts are bright green. Remove from heat immediately.
7. Lift the steamer out of the pan using tongs or wearing an oven mitt, and discard the water.
8. Dump the cooked sprouts back into the hot pan.

STEP TWO: LAYER THE FLAVOR

1. Mix together the oil, honey and vinegar in a jar with a lid and shake to emulsify.
2. Immediately pour the oil, honey and vinegar mixture into the hot sprouts, stir to coat.
3. Add the chopped walnuts, and stir to mix well.
4. Taste and season with salt and pepper to taste.
5. Serve hot as a side dish or cold as part of a salad.

Once upon a time

Brussels sprouts were popular in ancient Rome and then disappeared for centuries. In the 13th century, Dutch traders brought them back to Venice from Belgium, that's how they got their name. Venetians couldn't get enough of these little cabbages. They were Tavi's favorite cool season veggie. The secret to sweet sprouts is, don't over cook them!

ROASTED VEGETABLES WITH GREMOLATA

Adapted from a recipe contributed by Chef Allan King.

MAKE SURE TO READ THE WHOLE RECIPE BEFORE YOU START!
Serves 8 as a side dish

INGREDIENTS

- 1 pound carrots, washed
- 1 pound parsnips, washed
- 1 pound turnips, washed, peeled and cut in half
- 1½ pounds Brussels sprouts, ends trimmed, washed and cut in half
- ½ pound shallots, peeled and cut in half
- 4 tablespoons olive oil, divided *
- Salt and fresh ground pepper
- 1 lemon, washed well
- ¾ cup raw shelled walnuts
- ¼ cup Romano-Pecorino cheese, grated
- ¼ cup flat-leaf parsley leaves only, minced
- 1 clove garlic, minced

Collect and measure all of your ingredients to create a mise en place. Preheat the oven to 425°F.

STEP ONE: ROAST THE VEGETABLES

1. Cut the carrots and parsnips in half lengthwise and again crosswise.
2. Cut the turnips halves into 1-inch wedges.
3. Place the carrots, parsnips, turnips, Brussels sprouts and shallots in a large bowl. Drizzle with tablespoons of the oil. Toss to combine.
4. Line a sheet pan with foil and arrange the vegetables in one layer on top of the foil, sprinkle with salt and ground black pepper.
5. Place the sheet pan in the oven. Roast the vegetables for 50 minutes or until tender and nicely browned.
6. Remove sheet pan from the oven. Transfer the vegetables to a large platter; cover to keep warm.

STEP TWO: MAKE THE *GREMOLATA*

1. Grate the yellow peel (the zest) of the lemon with a grater or a microplane until you have accumulated a tablespoon. Avoid the bitter white part, (the pith).
2. Cut the lemon in half. Squeeze the juice into a bowl and remove the seeds.
3. Place the walnuts in a jar chopper and coarsely chop.
4. Transfer the walnuts to a bowl. Add all of the cheese, parsley, garlic and lemon zest, plus 1 tablespoon of lemon juice and 1 tablespoon of oil. Stir to combine.

STEP THREE: SERVE IT UP

1. Spread the *gremolata* evenly over the warm vegetables and gently toss to coat.

* When an ingredient says *divided* next to it, that means that a little bit will be used in one step of the recipe and the rest will be used in another part.

get adventurous!

Change up the vegetables you use according to the seasons. Cauliflower, winter squash and broccoli are all yummy with gremolata.

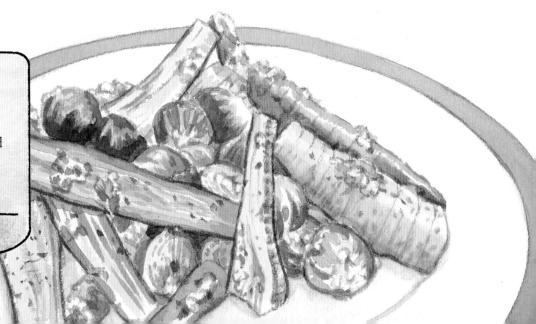

SPRING SALAD IN BLOOM

SOME IDEAS FOR EDIBLE FLOWERS TO USE IN YOUR SALAD

Borage or *Starflower*-sweet honey flavor

Carnations-sweet

Chrysanthemums-tangy

Cornflower or *Bachelor Button*-sweet, spicy clove like flavor

Dandelions-when picked young, they are sweet honey like; fully mature flowers are bitter

Daisy-pretty and edible, but bitter, so best for garnish

Fuchsia-acidic

Nasturtiums-peppery and sweet

Hibiscus-cranberry flavor with citrus notes

Honeysuckle-sweet honey flavor

Impatiens-very sweet

Marigolds-range from tangy to peppery to citrus

Pansy-grassy

Queen Anne's Lace-carrot flavor

Roses-sweet with strawberry and green apple top notes ranging from citrus to mint to spice

Tulips-sweet lettuce or cucumber

Violets-sweet perfumed flavor

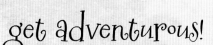

get adventurous!

Did you know that so many flowers are edible? They are perfect to use in salads to dress them up with color and add lots of vitamins.

tavi's tip

Tavi says "You can also use any flower from an herb, fruit or vegetable plant. There are many beautiful and tasty ones. Just remember, when you pick the flower from a plant, it won't produce as many fruits or vegetables. But when you pick an herb flower, it encourages the plant to put out more leaves."

MAKE SURE TO READ THE WHOLE RECIPE BEFORE YOU START!
Serves 2

INGREDIENTS

- 1 garlic clove, minced
- 1 green onion, minced
- ½ lemon
- 1 tablespoon sherry vinegar
- 1 tablespoon honey
- ¼ cup olive oil
- pinch of salt and fresh ground pepper to taste
- 1 cup loosely packed flowers or flower petals, gently washed and spun in a salad spinner or laid on paper towel to dry, plus 4 whole flowers reserved for garnish
- 3 cups loosely packed baby greens and herbs washed, stems removed, spun dry in a salad spinner and torn into bite-sized pieces or leaves

STEP ONE: MAKE THE DRESSING

1. Mince garlic and green onion. Place in a jar with tight fitting lid.
2. Cut lemon in half. Squeeze juice into the jar.
3. Add the vinegar and honey.
4. Pour in the olive oil.
5. Put the lid on the jar and shake it hard until the dressing is emulsified.

STEP TWO: DRESS THE BOWL

1. Pour dressing into a large serving bowl or wooden salad bowl, if you have one, and swirl it around to coat the bottom and sides of the bowl. Or you can use any large serving bowl.

STEP THREE: TOSS AND SERVE

1. Add flowers, greens and herbs into the bowl, and using your hands, gently toss to coat with dressing.
2. Divide equally onto individual salad plates and garnish with a whole flower and sprinkles of fresh cracked pepper.

HOMEMADE YOGURT

MAKE SURE TO READ THE WHOLE RECIPE BEFORE YOU START!

INGREDIENTS

- 1 quart + 3 tablespoons whole milk at room temperature, divided
- 3 tablespoons plain commercial yogurt with live cultures at room temperature (or from the last homemade batch you prepared)

STEP ONE: COOK AND COOL IT

1. Collect and measure all of your ingredients to create a *mise en place*.
2. In a large stockpot, bring 1 quart of milk to a boil, then turn down heat and simmer for two minutes.
3. Place pan in the sink or a large metal bowl filled with ice. Make sure none of the ice gets into the pan. Let it cool there until you can hold your clean finger in it for a count to ten. Or, use a thermometer and watch the temperature go down to 104°F.

STEP TWO: CURE IT

1. Stir 1 tablespoon of commercial yogurt into 3 tablespoons of room temperature milk in a medium glass bowl. You can do this while the boiled milk is cooling off.
2. Add the cooled, cooked milk into the glass bowl and stir.
3. Cover with plastic wrap, and then wrap the whole bowl in a heavy dish or bath towel.
4. Put in an unheated oven (make sure the oven is turned off) and leave it there for 8-12 hours.
5. Unwrap the bowl, and stir the yogurt. It should be thick and creamy.
6. Pour yogurt into a refrigerator container with a tight fitting lid. It will last 4-5 days. If you want to make it Greek Style, follow the steps for **TURNING PLAIN YOGURT INTO GREEK STYLE YOGURT, THE EASY WAY**.

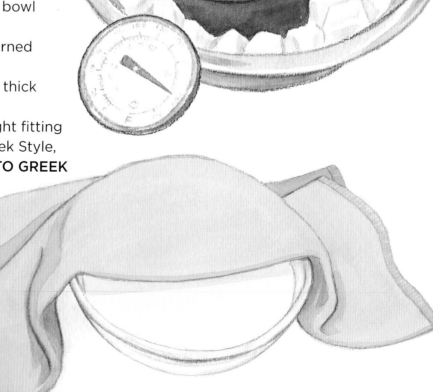

GREEK YOGURT

Turning Plain Yogurt into Greek Style Yogurt, the easy way.
MAKE SURE TO READ THE WHOLE RECIPE BEFORE YOU START!

INGREDIENTS

- 1 quart plain unflavored yogurt, homemade or store bought

STEP ONE: THE SOAK

1. Pour the plain yogurt into a colander lined with several layers of sterilized cheesecloth.
   Lay some cheesecloth on top to protect and let the moisture from the yogurt drip into the sink or a big pot for two hours.

STEP TWO: THE SQUEEZE

1. Lift the cheesecloth out and twist it to form the yogurt into a ball then gently squeeze the ball to remove the rest of the liquid.
2. Carefully dump the thickened yogurt into a refrigerator container with a tight-fitting lid.
3. Refrigerate for up to two weeks.

O*nce upon a time*
In Greek villages "yoghurt" is sold in clay pots or in goatskin bags.

TZATZIKI

MAKE SURE TO READ THE WHOLE RECIPE BEFORE YOU START!
Makes 16 ounces

Refreshing and smooth, this tangy dip is perfect with grilled meats and vegetables or simply served with pita bread triangles for dipping. It is the traditional sauce for **KALAMAKI** (recipe on page 100).

INGREDIENTS

- 3 tablespoons olive oil
- 1 tablespoon plain vinegar or lemon juice
- 2 cloves garlic, minced finely
- ½ teaspoon salt
- ¼ teaspoon white pepper
- 2 cups Greek yogurt
- 2 cucumbers, peeled, seeded and diced
- 1 teaspoon chopped fresh dill

STEP ONE: MIX IT UP

1. Collect and measure all of you ingredients to create a *mise en place*.
2. Combine olive oil, vinegar, garlic, salt and pepper in a medium bowl; stir with a fork to blend.
3. Add the yogurt to the olive oil mixture and stir well.
4. Add the cucumber and chopped fresh dill and stir again to completely blend.

STEP TWO: BUILD THE FLAVOR

1. Chill for at least 2 hours to infuse the flavor.
2. Store in a refrigerator container with a tight-fitting lid. Don't freeze it.

tavi's tip
This will keep covered in your refrigerator for up to two weeks.

KALAMAKI

Kalamaki *(little reed)* is also called souvlaki. It is a shish-ka-bob that is traditionally made from lamb cooked over an open fire.
Try this with chicken or pork—it's just as yummy!

MAKE SURE TO READ THE WHOLE RECIPE BEFORE YOU START!
Serves 6 as an entrée or main dish

INGREDIENTS

- ½ cup lemon juice
- ½ cup olive oil
- 2 tablespoons oregano leaves, minced
- 1½ pound lamb, cut into bite-sized cubes
- 1 whole lemon washed and cut into wedges
- tzatziki sauce (recipe on page 98)
- 6-12 fresh pitas

STEP ONE: MARINATE

1. Collect and measure all of your ingredients to create a *mise e place*.
2. Whisk together the lemon juice, olive oil and oregano in a medium bowl.
3. Add the cubes of meat and stir to completely coat and thoroughly mixed.
4. Cover the bowl and put in the refrigerator for 8-24 hours.

STEP TWO: COOK

1. Preheat the oven to broil.
2. Adjust top rack of oven to 4 inches below the top coils.
3. Carefully thread 6 pieces of meat on each of six wooden skewers. Scoot them close together so that there is no skewer showing in between the pieces.
4. Lay the skewers side by side on a roasting pan.
5. Put pan in oven. Leave the door slightly open and cook for 4-5 minutes until the meat browns. Keep a close eye on it so it doesn't burn.
6. Slide the rack out and using tongs, turn each skewer over.
7. Cook the other side 4-5 minutes or until it is browned.
8. Remove and serve immediately.

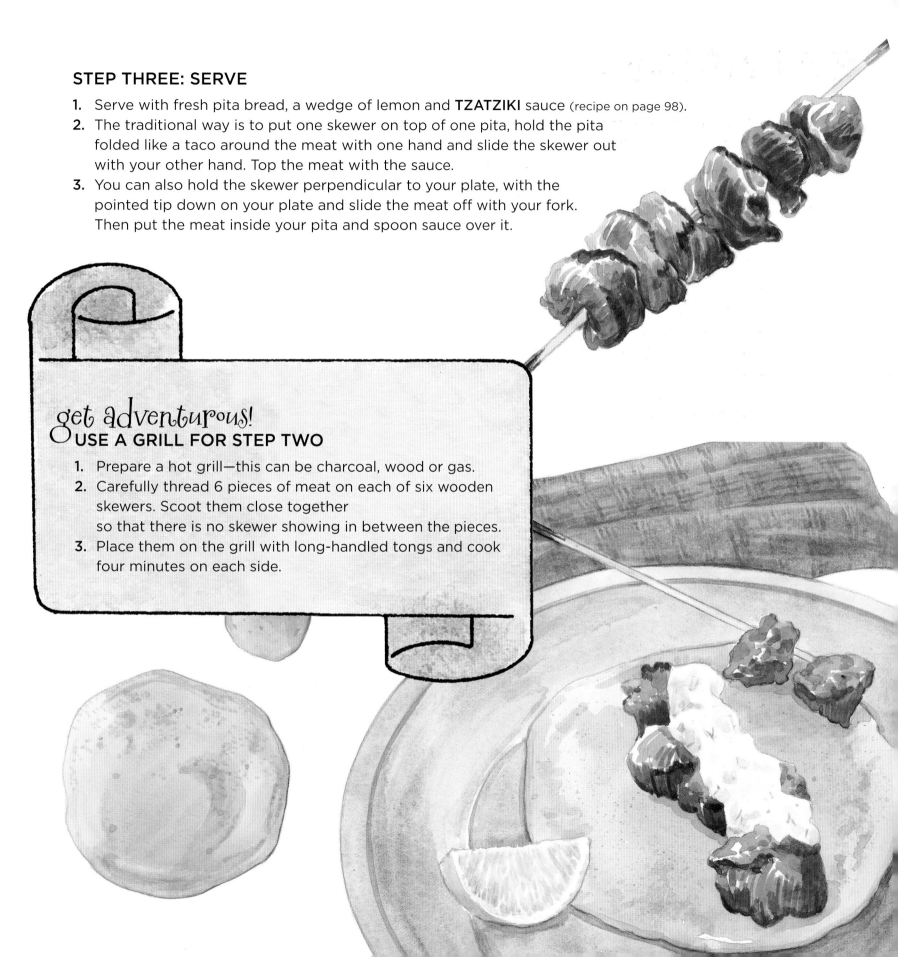

STEP THREE: SERVE

1. Serve with fresh pita bread, a wedge of lemon and **TZATZIKI** sauce (recipe on page 98).
2. The traditional way is to put one skewer on top of one pita, hold the pita folded like a taco around the meat with one hand and slide the skewer out with your other hand. Top the meat with the sauce.
3. You can also hold the skewer perpendicular to your plate, with the pointed tip down on your plate and slide the meat off with your fork. Then put the meat inside your pita and spoon sauce over it.

get adventurous!
USE A GRILL FOR STEP TWO

1. Prepare a hot grill—this can be charcoal, wood or gas.
2. Carefully thread 6 pieces of meat on each of six wooden skewers. Scoot them close together so that there is no skewer showing in between the pieces.
3. Place them on the grill with long-handled tongs and cook four minutes on each side.

FETA & VEGGIE ROLL UPS

Adapted from a recipe contributed by Chef Lance Fegan.
MAKE SURE TO READ THE WHOLE RECIPE BEFORE YOU START!
Serves 8 as an entrée or main dish

INGREDIENTS

- 8 pita breads, warmed
- 3 stems fresh oregano, leaves removed and stems discarded
- 1½ lbs feta cheese
- ½ - ¾ cup skim milk
- 2-3 cloves garlic
- 1 teaspoon black pepper, divided *
- 1 large English (seedless) cucumber
- 1 red bell pepper
- 1 small red onion
- 1 tablespoon olive oil
- ½ teaspoon kosher salt (or regular salt)
- 8 sprigs fresh mint

STEP ONE: PREPARE THE CHEESE

1. Collect and measure all of your ingredients to create a *mise en place*.
2. Chop the fresh oregano.
3. Peel and mince the garlic.
4. Place the cheese, ½ cup milk, oregano, and garlic in a food processor (or blender).
5. Purée until smooth (add a bit more milk if needed).
6. Season with pepper to taste.

* When an ingredient says *divided* next to it, that means that a little bit will be used in one step of the recipe and the rest will be used in another part.

STEP TWO: THE VEGGIES

1. Cut the cucumber into thin strips (called *julienne*)
2. Cut the red bell pepper in half. Remove stem, seeds, and ribs. Cut into julienne.
3. Peel and chop the red onion into small pieces.
4. Place the vegetables into a bowl. Add olive oil, salt and pepper. Toss to combine.

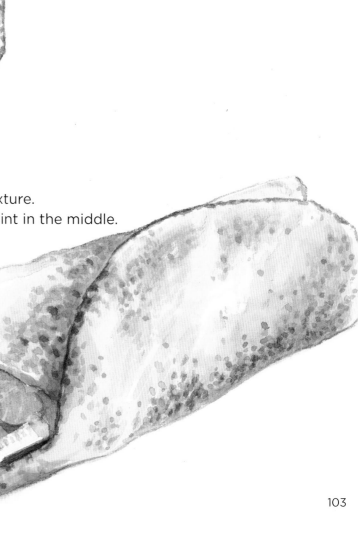

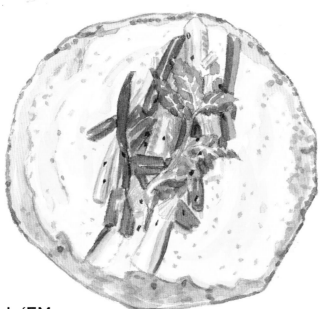

STEP THREE: ROLL 'EM

1. Smear each warm pita with a thick layer of the feta cheese mixture.
2. Place the vegetables on top of the cheese and lay a sprig of mint in the middle.
3. Roll up the pita. Enjoy!

FISH SOUP

It's easy and fast to make a simple fish soup with any seasonal vegetables that you have on hand.

MAKE SURE TO READ THE WHOLE RECIPE BEFORE YOU START!

INGREDIENTS

The ingredients listed are for each serving (multiply by the number of servings you need)

For one serving:

- 1 carrot, split in quarters lengthwise, then cut into 2-inch pieces
- 1 stalk of celery, sliced lengthwise into thin strips, then cut into 2-inch pieces
- 1 leek, white part only, sliced in quarters lengthwise, then cut into 2-inch pieces
- 2 small red potatoes cut into quarters
- 1 handful of chopped fresh greens—spinach, chard, and/or kale
- 1 cup broth (vegetable or chicken)
- 3-4 ounces firm white fish filet—cod, drum, pike, or tilapia
- 1 sprig of fresh thyme or tarragon
- Sea salt and ground black pepper

STEP ONE: ASSEMBLE VEGGIES

1. Collect and measure all of your ingredients to create a *mise en place*.
2. Select a sauté pan with a lid that is the right size to hold the number of servings you are preparing: a small pan for 1-2 servings, a medium pan for 4-6 servings or a large pan for up to 8 servings.
3. Layer vegetables in your pan, ending in greens.
4. Pour in just enough broth to come to bottom of the greens (about an inch).
5. Over medium heat, bring broth to a simmer.
6. Turn heat to low, put the lid on, cook for 10 minutes.

STEP TWO: ADD FISH

1. Lay fish filet on top of the greens.
2. Add sprig of thyme or tarragon on top of fish.
3. Cover and cook for 6 minutes longer.

STEP THREE: SERVE

1. Slide a spatula under the cooked fish and veggies and lift into a big shallow bowl.
2. Spoon extra veggies and broth on top.
3. Season with sea salt and freshly ground pepper to taste.

tavi's tip
You can add seasonal vegetables like chopped broccoli, green beans or cauliflower.

desserts

PEARS & CINNAMON

MAKE SURE TO READ THE WHOLE RECIPE BEFORE YOU START!
Serves 4

INGREDIENTS

- 4 medium pears, peeled, quartered lengthwise, seeds removed
- 2 tablespoons freshly squeezed lemon juice
- 2 tablespoons honey
- 1 teaspoon vanilla
- 1 teaspoon ground cinnamon
- ¼ teaspoon ground nutmeg
- 1 tablespoon canola oil
- ¼ cup plain yogurt

STEP ONE: LAYER THE FLAVOR

1. Collect and measure all of your ingredients to create a *mise en place*.
2. In a medium bowl, combine lemon juice, honey, vanilla, cinnamon and nutmeg.
3. Add the pears and gently toss to coat on all sides being careful not to break any.

STEP TWO: COOK

1. In a skillet, heat oil over medium heat.
2. Lay pears quarters on their sides in the skillet in one layer and cook for 3 minutes or until they start to turn a little brown.
3. Use a spatula or tongs to gently turn the pears to the other side and cook for 2-3 more minutes until that side starts to brown.
4. Pour the reserved cinnamon liquid into the warm pan; stir and cook until it thickens. Be careful! Don't let it burn!

STEP THREE: SERVE

1. Gently lift pears out onto four individual dessert plates and arrange like a fan.
2. Garnish with a dollop of fresh yogurt and sprinkle of cinnamon.
3. Carefully drizzle the cinnamon sauce on top and serve warm.

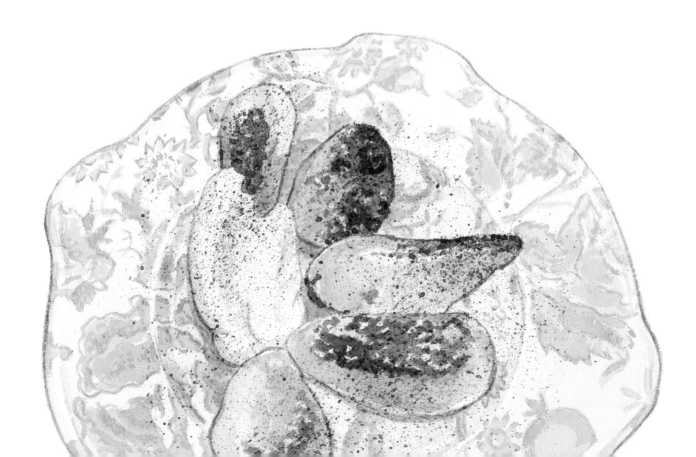

SAFFRON & FIG CAKE

MAKE SURE TO READ THE WHOLE RECIPE BEFORE YOU START!
Serves 9-12

INGREDIENTS

- 1 teaspoon + ¾ cup softened unsalted butter, divided *
- 1½ cups all-purpose flour
- ¼ cup almonds, finely ground
- 1½ teaspoons baking powder
- pinch of salt
- ¼ cup skim milk
- ½ teaspoon saffron threads
- ¾ cup honey
- 3 large eggs
- zest of 1 lemon
- ⅛ teaspoon pure almond extract
- ¼ cup almonds, chopped
- 1 pint of fresh figs, sliced lengthwise into quarters

STEP ONE: PREPARE

1. Collect and measure all of your ingredients to create a *mise en place*.
2. Preheat oven to 350°F.
3. Smear a thin coating of butter onto the bottom and sides of a 9-inch square, glass baking dish. Set aside.
4. In a small bowl, sift together all the dry ingredients: flour, ground almonds, baking powder, and salt and set aside.
5. In a small saucepan, combine the milk and saffron threads and cook over medium low heat until it starts to simmer, then immediately remove. (This can also be done in a glass measuring cup in the microwave for 30 seconds set on high.)
6. Allow the saffron to steep in the milk as it cools for about 15 minutes while you start **STEP TWO**. The milk will turn a rich yellow color.

* *tavi's note*
When an ingredient says *divided* next to it, that means that a little bit will be used in one step of the recipe and the rest will be used in another part.

STEP TWO: LAYER THE FLAVOR

1. Add ¾ cup of softened butter and the honey to a medium mixing bowl.
2. Beat with electric mixer on high for about 3 minutes, until light and fluffy.
3. Add the eggs to the bowl one at a time and beat well to incorporate each one before adding the next.
4. Add cooled milk and saffron, lemon zest and almond extract to the egg and butter mixture, and beat on high for 2 minutes. *Don't worry if the batter looks curdled.*
5. With the mixer on the lowest speed, slowly add the dry ingredients to the wet ones and mix until everything is well blended. The batter will be thick.

STEP THREE: BAKE

1. Cover the bottom of the baking dish with a solid layer of chopped almonds.
2. Arrange the figs on top of the almonds to completely cover the bottom. They can even be stacked on top of each other a little bit in order to use them all.
3. Gently pour the batter over the figs and smooth out the top all the way to the edges of the pan.
4. Bake in oven for 45 minutes to 1 hour, or until a toothpick inserted into the center of the cake comes out clean.

Enjoy warm or cooled with a dollop of plain yogurt on top!

get adventurous!

This cake can be made with whole-wheat flour, but skip the saffron because its delicate flavor will be overwhelmed. Instead add a second fruit. Experiment with different combinations of fruit. Try plums or peaches. You can even try mixing in some dried fruit, like cherries, but just 1/4 cup or the cake will be too sweet. You might try swapping out the almonds for walnuts. If you do that, then also switch the almond extract to vanilla.

FRUIT & HONEY BUNDLES

These are great served warm right out of the oven for dessert, but they also work at room temperature, packed for lunch or as an afternoon snack.

MAKE SURE TO READ THE WHOLE RECIPE BEFORE YOU START!
Serves 12

INGREDIENTS

- 1 recipe **BASIC WHOLE WHEAT FLATBREAD** (recipe on page 54)
  MAKE THIS ADJUSTMENT TO THE FLATBREAD RECIPE:
  Add 2 tablespoons of honey just before you knead it and before allowing the Flatbread to rise
- 2 tablespoons light brown sugar
- 1 tablespoon whole wheat flour
- ¼ teaspoon ground nutmeg
- 4 tablespoons honey, divided ✳
- 2 mediums apples—select one sweet apple like Pink Lady and one tart like Granny Smith, peeled and chopped into ½ inch dice
- ¼ cup raisins or chopped dates
- 1 cup fresh cherries, pits removed
- 1 tablespoon walnuts, finely chopped
- 1 tablespoon sugar-in-the-raw

STEP ONE: PREPARE THE BUNDLES

1. Preheat the oven to 350°F.
2. Collect and measure all of your ingredients to create a *mise en place*.
3. Spray or wipe a thin film of oil into the cups of a 12-cup muffin pan.
4. Punch down the flat bread dough and divide it into 12 small balls.
5. Lightly flour your work surface.
6. One by one, roll the dough ball in flour so that it isn't sticky, then flatten it.
7. With a rolling pin, roll the flattened ball into a round disc about 6 inches in diameter and very thin— ⅛ inch or so.
8. Gently lay the dough disc into a muffin cup and carefully press it into the sides and bottom of the cup. It will spill out and overlap the edges of the cup.

✳ When an ingredient says *divided* next to it, that means that a little bit will be used in one step of the recipe and the rest will be used in another part.

STEP TWO: MAKE THE FILLING

1. Combine the sugar, flour, and nutmeg in a medium bowl and stir to mix well.
2. Dump in the apples, cherries and dried fruit, stir until they are well coated.
3. In a separate small bowl, combine 1 tablespoon of honey and the walnuts.

STEP THREE: PACK THE BUNDLE

1. Beginning with the last muffin tin cup you filled with dough, spoon ¼ cup of fruit into the middle and then add ½ teaspoon of honey on top of the fruit. (You can just squirt from bottle and estimate the amount.)
2. Fold the dough edges to the middle so that they overlap each other and cover the filling, like wrapping a bundle.
3. Repeat with each muffin cup. If you work backwards, it will be easy to get to the outside edges of each dough cup.
4. When all the Fruit Bundles are packed, top each with ⅛ teaspoon or so of the honey-nut mixture.
5. Lightly sprinkle each bundle with a pinch of sugar-in-the-raw.
6. Bake for 25-30 minutes until the bundles' tops are browned and the filling is bubbly.
7. Remove from oven, cool slightly and serve warm with a scoop of fresh or frozen yogurt.

get adventurous!

Think of other fruits to add to the apples in place of cherries. Anything that's in season works.

YIAOURTI ME MELI

(Yogurt with Honey) Pronounced (yee-ah-OOR-tee meh MEH-lee)

In many Greek restaurants, this dessert is served compliments of the house because yogurt and honey are great for good digestion. Either use commercial Greek yogurt or make your own.

MAKE SURE TO READ THE WHOLE RECIPE BEFORE YOU START!

INGREDIENTS

- ½-¾ cup Greek yogurt per serving
- 1-2 teaspoons Greek thyme honey per serving
- ¼ cup fresh fruit per serving. Use what is in season and, if necessary, cut into bite sized pieces
- 1 tablespoon crushed walnuts and/or almonds per serving
- 1 borage flower or other edible flower per serving

tavi's tip
Try it for breakfast!

PREPARATION

1. Collect and measure all of your ingredients to create a *mise en place*.
2. In individual serving bowls, drizzle honey over the yogurt, top with fruit and sprinkle with nuts.
3. Garnish with a blue borage flower, also known as starflower, or you can also use a rose, narcissus or any other edible flower. See the list of **EDIBLE FLOWERS** on page 94.

WHERE DID THIS COME FROM?

 ALMONDS
Native to the Middle East where they first appeared around 3000 BC, almonds were named by the Greeks and spread during ancient times along the shores of the Mediterranean into India and northern Africa, then to Europe.

 **ANCHOVY**
Used since at least the times of ancient Rome, anchovies are small, oily fish found in mild waters like the Indian Ocean and Mediterranean Sea that can be eaten cooked or dried but are usually canned in oil or packed in salt. Romans used them as a staple food for long-distance traveling, and almost every culture has a sauce made from some form of preserved anchovies.

 **APPLE**
Originating in eastern Turkey and may be the earliest tree to be cultivated, the apple is a member of the rose family. Greek and Roman mythology refer to apples as the symbols of love. Soldiers carried them throughout Europe during the expansion of the Roman Empire in 1st Century BC, and Europeans brought them to North America in the 1600s. There are now more than 7500 different kinds of apples.

 **ARTICHOKE**
Found in Egypt during the Roman period, cultivated in Sicily during the Greek occupation and in Naples in the mid 9th century, artichokes slowly made their way through northern Europe in the 15th and 16th centuries. They were brought to Louisiana by French settlers and to California by Spanish settlers in the 19th century.

 **ASPARAGUS**
Seen in an Egyptian frieze painted in 3000 BC, asparagus was cultivated by ancient Egyptians, Greeks and Romans who ate it fresh in the spring season and dried it to use through the rest of the year.

 **BANANA**
Originating in Papua, New Guinea as early as 5000 BCE, by the 10th century, bananas had appeared throughout growing regions in Southeast Asia, India, parts of the Middle East and Africa. Bananas spread across Europe after Islamic rulers conquered Iberia (present-day Spain) and were brought to America by Portuguese sailors.

 BARLEY
The first domesticated grain in the Near East around 8,000 BC, the wild version dates as far back as 8500 BC near the Sea of Galilee and was found from North Africa and Crete to Tibet. Roman gladiators considered it a special

food, but by the Middle Ages bread made from barley was considered peasant food, and the upper classes ate wheat products.

BASIL

Original to the Middle East, where it has been cultivated since 3000 BC, basil is prominent in Italian and Southeast Asian cuisines.

BLACK PEPPER

Thought to be original to Indonesia, black pepper was grown along India's Malabar Coast, which was the primary source until well after the Middle Ages. Referred to as black gold and used instead of money, black pepper launched the discovery of the New World, as explorers looked for a faster route to India.

BORAGE

An annual plant that can be used as a fresh vegetable or dried herb, borage originated in Syria. The leaves have a cucumber taste and its star shaped blue flowers taste like honey. It commonly added to soup, but Northern Italians used it as a traditional filling for ravioli.

BROCCOLI

Cultivated for more than 2,000 years, broccoli was a popular vegetable in the Roman Empire. Italian immigrants first brought it to the United States, but it took until 1920 for other Americans to accept it.

BROWN SUGAR

Most commercially available brown sugar is made from refined white sugar with the addition of molasses. Natural brown sugar or raw sugar has a higher mineral content than highly processed white sugar. It is produced from the first crystal-lization of sugar cane. Turbinado, Muscovado and Demerara are all natural brown sugars.

BRUSSELS SPROUTS

The ancestors to present day Brussels sprouts were grown in ancient Rome, but emerged in the present form in 13th century. Netherlands and Dutch traders spread them throughout Europe.

BUTTERMILK

Originally buttermilk was what was left when butter was churned out of cream; adding lactic acid bacteria to whole cow's milk creates cultured buttermilk on purpose.

CARROTS

The ancestors to our cultivated carrots grew wild in Afghanistan. They were originally cultivated for their aromatic seeds and leaves. The root was first used in the 1st century, and by the 12th century Arabs were cultivating red and yellow varieties. Orange carrots popular today showed up in the Netherlands in the 17th century. You can eat the leaves and stems, but hardly anyone does anymore.

WHERE DID THIS COME FROM?
(continued)

CELERY
Originally from the Middle East, celery was named by the Mycenaean Greeks in 12th century BC. It was referred to by Homer in both the Iliad and the Odyssey— written around 8th century BC, was found in the tomb of pharaoh Tutankhamen who died in 1323 BC, and was used by the Romans as medicine in 30 AD. By the 17th century it had spread throughout the kitchens of Europe. The leaves were used in salads, the stalks in soups and the seeds as a spice.

CHERRIES
Brought from Turkey in 72 BC to Rome, cherries were exported throughout the Roman Empire. King Henry VIII tasted them in Flanders and brought them to England in the 16th century.

CINNAMON
Cinnamon trees are native to Sri Lanka, and the spice is made from its inner bark. To produce great quantities, a 2-year old tree is cut off at the base to stimulate re-growth of dozens of small branches, which are harvested. The outer bark of these small branches is scraped off and then the very thin inner bark is removed in 30-36 inch long strips that curl into tight rolls when they dry. After about 6 hours, when they are completely dry, the long rolls are cut into short sticks, 2-3 inches long.

The spice was highly prized among the monarchs of ancient nations and considered a gift worthy of Apollo. It was exported to Egypt as early as 2000 BC, where Alexandria was a major shipping center for the spice trade. The men who controlled the Spice Route kept cinnamon's origins a secret for centuries to protect their business, so many myths were promoted about its origin, including a story about how it was collected from an unknown land by giant Cinnamon birds to build their nests. In fact, Indonesians took it by boat from Moluccas to East Africa, where Arab traders took it overland to Alexandria, where Venetian traders bought it. Venetians held a monopoly on the spice trade to Europe. Then Crusaders also brought it back to Europe in the 13th century. In the 16th century, Portuguese traders finally found their way to Sri Lanka and established a fort on the island, where they held a monopoly over the cinnamon trade for over 100 years. The Dutch took control in 1638, and the Dutch East India Company overhauled the entire cinnamon industry. 130 years later the British seized control. 90% of the world's cinnamon still comes from Sri Lanka.

COD
A flakey white cold-water fish with mild flavor, cod is high in vitamins A, D, E and Omega-3s.

CUCUMBERS
A fruit originating in India where it has been cultivated for over 3,000 years, cucumbers spread to ancient Greece and Italy and then to China. The Romans who grew them year-round in greenhouses introduced cucumbers to Europe. By the 9th century, they made it to France and by the 14th century, to England. Christopher Columbus brought cucumbers to Haiti in 1494. Romans not only ate them, they used them for bug bites, and medieval wives wishing for more children wore them around their waists.

DILL
Sprigs of dill were found in the tomb of pharaoh Amenhotep II and in Roman ruins as far north as Great Britain. The lacy aromatic leaves are used as herbs; the round seeds are used as a spice and the delicate yellow flowers are often used in pickling.

EGGS
In Southeast Asia and India, chickens were domesticated for their eggs as early as 7500 BC. They were brought to Egypt by 1500 BC and later to Greece in 800 BC. Before then, people ate foraged quail eggs. Ancient Romans developed a way to preserve eggs and made them a part of every meal, often as the first course.

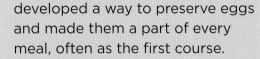

FETA
A brined curd cheese, Feta was developed on the island of Crete in the 1st century AD from cow's milk and became a strong Greek tradition that continues to this day. Now, it is mostly all made from sheep or goat's milk.

FIGS
Figs may have been the very first crop to be cultivated—even before grain. Remains have been found in the Jordan Valley in the Middle East that date from 9400 BC. They were a common food source in early civilizations and ancient Rome. They can be eaten fresh in season, but because they are so delicate, they are usually dried or made into jam for transport and for yearlong enjoyment. References to figs are woven throughout our civilization's stories from Greek mythology to the Bible and Quran. We think of figs as fruit, but they are actually flowers. They are extremely high in calcium.

FLATBREAD
Simple bread made from flour, water and salt, it only sometimes has a leaven. Since ancient Egypt, every culture has flatbread, each unique with different grains, spices, herbs and shapes.

WHERE DID THIS COME FROM?
(continued)

FOCACCIA
A flatbread containing generous portions of olive oil, focaccia originated from the ancient Etruscans. In the 13th century, it was adapted by bakers in Genoa, Italy and traditionally was made with sea salt and rosemary, although each family or village had its own signature topping. The style spread through France and Spain. Pizza is a form of focaccia.

GARLIC
Descended from a wild plant native to Southeast Asia, garlic was first cultivated in Egypt sometime between 500-400 BC. Peasants, soldiers and ruling classes through-out the Roman Empire consumed it and used it for medicinal purposes to cure everything from heat stroke to respiratory issues and poor digestion. Garlic is used generously in the cuisines of Mediterranean countries.

GINGER
Originally cultivated in Indonesia, ginger tubers can be used fresh or candied or powdered as a spice. It was first referred to in the 4th century BC in India and by 13th century and was one of the most commonly traded spices throughout countries of the former Roman Empire. Garlic was valued as a medicine and used in both sweet and savory cooking.

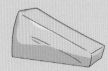

GRUYERE CHEESE
A hard yellow cheese made from cow's milk, Gruyère is sweet, tangy and a bit salty. It is named after a town in Switzerland, but popular varieties are made in Greece, Crete, and France.

HONEY
Made by bees from flower nectar, honey has long been gathered and used as a sweetener. The earliest references to honey gathering are in a Mesolithic rock painting, from nearly 10,000 yeas ago. It was used in ancient Egypt to sweeten food and for medicinal purposes. In the days of the Roman Empire, citizens could pay their taxes in honey instead of gold. Myths and stories about honey have been woven into the traditions of many cultures for centuries.

LAMB
The meat butchered from a sheep that is less than one year old is referred to as lamb. It is the dominant meat in Mediterranean cultures.

LETTUCE
Considered sacred by ancient Egyptians, pictures of lettuce were carved into Pharaoh Senusret's temple at Karnak in 1975 BC. The ancient Greeks believed lettuce could help you sleep. The ancient Romans grew it and spread its popularity throughout their empire.

LEEK
First appearing in ancient Egypt in the 1st century BC, the Roman Emperor Nero so famously enjoyed them in the 1st century AD, that he was nicknamed Porophagus (leek eater). Phoenician traders brought them to Wales before 640 AD, where leeks became so popular they became the national symbol.

LEMONS
First grown in India, Burma and China, lemons came to Italy in the 1st century AD and then spread to Persia and throughout the Middle East where they became widely cultivated and distributed throughout the Mediterranean.

LENTILS
Originated in India, lentils have been eaten since the New Stone Age in 9500 BC and were one of the first crops cultivated in the Near East.

MARJORAM
Often interchangeable with oregano, the sweet herb marjoram is indigenous to the Mediterranean area of the Middle East. It was a symbol of happiness to ancient Greeks and Romans. It can be used fresh or dried.

MOZZARELLA
A fresh, uncured Italian cheese made from cow or water buffalo milk by spinning and cutting, stretching and kneading it like bread.

MUSHROOMS
Thought by ancient Egyptians circa 2000 BC to ensure immortality, the pharaohs ordered that no commoner could touch these edible fungi.

NUTMEG
We only use the seed inside the fruit of a nutmeg tree. First found growing in Indonesia, the spice became very popular in Europe in the Middle Ages despite its extremely high price. Nutmeg instigated trade wars between the Dutch, British and French for control of the lucrative spice routes to Southeast Asia.

OLIVE OIL
Over 750 million olive trees are grown worldwide to satisfy the demand for this flavorful and healthy oil. Commercial olive production started in Crete before 4,000 BC, then became widespread throughout the Mediterranean region. In ancient Greece, Homer called it liquid gold.

ONIONS
Traces of onion have been found in Bronze Age stones dating as far back as 5,000 BC, but we think that people started growing them in ancient Egypt. The pyramid builders were fed a diet of radishes and onions, which was believed to have good effect on health.

WHERE DID THIS COME FROM?
(continued)

OREGANO
A perennial herb that is high in antioxidants, people have used it for cooking since the Middle Ages. It was grown throughout the Middle East and especially important in Turkish Persian and Greek kitchens.

PANCAKES
Invented in ancient Rome, this all-time favorite food was called Alita Dolcia, which is Latin for "another sweet." To this day almost every culture has its own variation using a wide range of flours.

PAPRIKA
First used in Turkish cooking in the middle ages, it was a Hungarian family that invented the machine to strip the stalks and seeds from paprika peppers and grind them into a powder.

PARMESAN CHEESE
Made from skimmed cow's milk, Parmesan cheese was developed in Parma, Italy in the 13th century and has become the king of Italian cheeses, beloved around the world.

PARSLEY
First mentioned by ancient Romans in the 4th century BC, parsley was used in salads throughout the Mediterranean. In the Middle Ages, it was used in centerpieces and even garlands to absorb food odors.

PARSNIPS
A relative of the carrot, parsnips originated in the Mediterranean. Soldiers of the Roman Empire were responsible for spreading them throughout Europe.

PASTA
When man learned how to mill grain, he began making pasta, and every culture developed its own style and shapes. Pasta can be made of flour and water or can have egg added. It can be cooked "fresh" or be dried and stored and then boiled. There are more than 320 different kinds and shapes of pasta in Italy, where it has been cooked since the 11th century. There are references to pasta in 2nd century Greek texts, and it has been eaten in China since 2000 BC. Layered and stuffed pasta are Medieval.

PEACHES
Native to Persia, peaches may have first been used as food in China where they were cultivated as early as 1100 BC. Alexander the Great introduced the peach to the West from Persia, and Spanish explorers brought it to the Americas.

PEARS
Pears have been eaten since pre-historic times and grown in China for more than 3000 years. Homer referred to pears in the Odyssey, and the early Romans cultivated them.

PEAS

Originally from Turkey, Syria and Jordan, peas date back to Neolithic times and were grown in the Nile delta of Egypt as early as 4800 BC

PINE NUTS

The seeds of pine trees are harvested from pinecones and called pine nuts. About twenty kinds of pine trees make edible nuts and people have used them for food since the Paleolithic period. High in vitamins and protein, they may also be an appetite suppressant.

PITA

A westernized name for traditional Arabic flat bread that puffs up with steam when it is cooked. As the bread cools, a pocket is left in the middle. Pita is used throughout Middle Eastern, Mediterranean and Northern African cooking and was referred to as early as the 10th century in an Arab cookbook.

RADISHES

Wild radishes are found all over China, West Asia and Europe, and we know they have been grown for food in Greece since about 3000 BC where they were very valuable. In fact the Greeks made small radish replicas in gold (beets were silver and turnips lead). They were a common food in Egypt even before the great Pyramids were built.

RASPBERRIES

Native to Turkey, raspberries have been gathered for food since the 1st century BC. Soldiers spread the seeds throughout the Roman Empire. They have been cultivated in Europe ever since and were brought to America in 1737.

RICE

One of the most important food crops in the world, rice was first grown in the Yangtze River valley of China as early as 12,000 BC, and spread very rapidly to the west by the Medieval times.

RICOTTA

A fresh cow's milk cheese ricotta is produced from whey (what's left after hard cheese is made). We think that Greek Pecorino Romano cheese makers in Sicily first discovered it in 750 BC.

ROSEMARY

The Greek goddess Aphrodite was draped in rosemary when she arose from the sea and this aromatic herb has been used for seasoning food, and for medicinal and celebration purposes throughout the centuries. In the middle ages, brides wore a rosemary crown.

WHERE DID THIS COME FROM?
(continued)

SAFFRON
Rare and expensive, saffron is made from the pistils of a crocus flower. Its has a complex aroma with more than 150 compounds and a golden orange color, which makes it valuable as a spice, a medicine and a dye. Saffron has been used in textiles, as offerings to gods, steeped as tea, to create perfumes, ground for cosmetics, even as a restorative bath. Highly prized for centuries, it has been cultivated for more than 3,000 years, but used for 50,000 years. Prehistoric cave paintings have been found in northern Iran that show saffron in use, and it has been traded long distance since before the 2nd millennium BC. Saffron was one of the most significant spices that drove the trade routes east to west and inspired centuries of exploration. You can buy it ground, or still in the pistils that look like deep orange threads.

SAGE
A perennial herb with a slightly peppery flavor, sage has been used since ancient times for warding off evil and curing snakebites. The Romans picked it up in Egypt and took it to Europe, and the Emperor Charlemagne was the first to encourage its cultivation in the Middle Ages. It was used for its healing powers and added to foods, especially meats.

SCALLION OR GREEN ONION
Originally used in Israel in 300 BC, scallions are the mildest of the onion family.

SEA SALT
Different from table salt, which is a mined mineral, sea salt is made by evaporating seawater. It has been produced throughout the Mediterranean region in coastal areas and salt marshes since the time of the Roman Empire.

SESAME SEED
The flowering sesame plant is an annual, native to sub-Saharan Africa, but it was first cultivated in India and Pakistan between 2250 and 1750 BC. The seeds grow in pods that burst open when they mature. They can be crushed for oil or eaten whole—either raw or roasted.

SHALLOT
A sweet, mild member of the onion family, shallots originated in Asia and traveled via India to the eastern Mediterranean well before the time of the Classic Greeks, in the 8th century BC.

SOUR CREAM
Romans first used cream in the 9th century. Since then, we have had sour cream, which initially occurred naturally when cream was left too long in the heat. Frugal cultures made something of it. Similar to yogurt, sour cream

became popular in sauces used in central and northern Europe, and was often used as a substitute for milk in baking.

SPINACH
Originally from Persia, spinach migrated to China in the 7th century when the king of Nepal sent it as a gift. The Chinese called the leafy green vegetable the "Herb of Persia." It made its way into Italian kitchens in the 11th century and was Catherine de Medici's favorite food. When she left Florence, Italy in the 16th century to marry King Henry II of France, she brought both spinach and cooks who knew her favorite ways to eat it. Ever since, dishes that are served on a bed of spinach are called "a la Florentine."

STRAWBERRY
The symbol for Venus, their goddess of love, ancient Romans believed that strawberries cured all sorts of ailments. Wild strawberries are the only fruit with seeds on the outside, and are widespread thanks to being a favorite of migrating birds. The popular fruit has been depicted in stories, literature and paintings since around 150 AD.

SUMAC
A tart red berry that grows in tight clusters, appearing on trees in late summer and early fall. First used by the ancient Greeks, sumac has been popular throughout the Mediterranean region to make tea, used in place of lemon, and ground to add as a flavoring for over 2,000 years.

SWISS CHARD
Despite its name, this member of the beet family was first referred to by Aristotle in the 4th century BC and was popular throughout Greek and Early Roman times for its medicinal power.

TAHINI
A paste made from ground sesame seeds, tahini originated in ancient Persia. It is now a common Middle Eastern ingredient.

TARRAGON
Named for its snaky root system, early Greeks and Romans thought that tarragon cured snakebites. The licorice-flavored perennial herb is native to the Middle East, India and Eastern Europe and has been used for medicine and cooking for centuries.

WHERE DID THIS COME FROM?
(continued)

THYME
Ancient Egyptians used thyme for embalming. The Greeks burned it as incense and added it to their baths because they thought it gave them courage. By the Middle Ages people put it under their pillows to help them sleep without nightmares. It is used frequently in cooking through-out the Middle East and Mediterra-nean regions of Europe.

TURNIPS
Even though wild turnips are found all over Asia and Europe, we don't know for sure where they came from. We do know they have been cultivated since ancient Greek and Roman times. Both the roots and leaves are used.

VANILLA
This is the only ingredient included in this book that was not known to Tavi and his family in Italy during the Middle Ages. We could have substituted something else for authenticity, but our cakes and pancakes are so much better with it, we just didn't want to. Vanilla was first cultivated by the Totonac people on the gulf coast of what is now the country of Mexico long before the 15th century. It comes from a special kind of orchid plant and must be cured.

VINEGAR
Vinegar has been used for medicine since the time of Hippocrates in the 5th century BC. Traces have been found in Egyptian urns from 3000 BC, and the Chinese began using it as a condiment in 2000 BC.

WALNUTS
Even though they have been found in early cave drawings, the first people to cultivate walnuts were the Babylonians in 2000 BC. To this day, the most popular walnut is the Persian Walnut, which the Romans planted all over Europe and North Africa.

WHITE PEPPER
(see Black Pepper) White pepper is made from the berries of pepper fruit with the dark outer skin removed. A slightly milder pepper, it is used in light colored sauces and foods for appearance sake, but also where a more delicate flavor is desired.

YOGURT
Used for at least 5,400 years, yogurt was first referred to in writing by the famous Roman historian, Pliny the Elder, and in an 11th century Turkish cookbook.

A NOTE ABOUT FLOUR & BREAD

HISTORY OF FLOUR AND BREAD

Bread is the single most important food to mankind. Through the ages, many references to bread reflect its importance to us, including referring to money as bread. References used in western civilization include: Bread is the staff of life, bread winner, putting bread on the table, the best thing since sliced bread, and agricultural breadbasket. In Arabic, the slang for bread is "*ayish*," which means "the constellation," in other words the whole world. In India, it's said that life's necessities are "*roti, kapra aur makan,*" which means "bread, cloth and house." In the 13th century, one of the first laws ever written was for the sale of bread.

The increase of the world's population can be tied directly to the cultivation and processing of wheat. 10,000 years ago, when nomads stopped roaming and planted something to grow for food, it was wheat. At first they just chewed on the seeds. Then, they began grinding the seeds by hand on stones, and then they added water to make cereal. At some point, the cereal ended up over a fire, making hard, flat bread that could keep for several days. Yeast was probably discovered by accident, too. Around 1000 BC, the Egyptians were the first to use yeast on purpose to make bread.

The ancient Egyptians produced over thirty varieties of yeast bread. The Greeks learned from the Egyptians. The Romans learned from the Greeks, and their bread making spread along ancient trade routes and throughout the Roman Empire as it expanded. To grind wheat, the Romans originally used large wheels turned by animals or slaves. Around 25 BC the Romans began using a paddlewheel moved by water to turn the stone grinder. In the Middle Ages around 1100, Europeans started using windmills to turn the stones. Windmills were used for more than 600 years until the start of the Industrial Age. In 1786, the first steam mill was built in Britain on the banks of the River Thames.

Today, industrial mills around the world process over 320 million tons of wheat, which is the primary food for more than a third of the world's population.

So, the largest food crop in the world is wheat, and the most common flour is made from wheat. But flour can also be ground from any grain, or from nuts, roots and other plants. Every country has its favorites and specialties, which are tied to local agricultural practices. Look for flour made from barley, rice, corn, oats, almonds, peanuts, tapioca, potato and dozens of other sources.

There are six primary classes of wheat that most flour is made from: Hard Red Winter, Hard Red Spring, Soft Red Winter, Hard White, Soft White and Durhum.

The biggest difference between wheat flours is protein content, which determines the gluten. (See the science of bread, next page.) The harder the wheat, the more protein the flour has. It stacks up this way:

SEMINOLA
13-16% protein; made from Durham, the very hardest type of wheat grown. The gluten formed is less elastic than with other flour, and it is better for pasta than for bread.

BREAD FLOUR
12-15% protein; made from Hard Winter Red Wheat.

WHOLE WHEAT FLOUR
14% protein; made from Hard Red Spring Wheat; also contains the embryo of the wheat kernel and has more nutrients, fiber and fat than more processed flour. Whole Wheat flour needs more water for the proteins to form gluten.

WHITE WHOLE WHEAT
14% protein; made from Hard White Spring Wheat; also contains the embryo of the wheat kernel and has more nutrients, fiber and fat than more processed flour. Hard White Wheat has a milder flavor than Hard Red Wheat. All Whole Wheat flours needs more water for the proteins to form gluten.

ALL PURPOSE FLOUR
10-12% protein; mixes Hard Winter Red Wheat and Soft Summer Red Wheat

PASTRY FLOUR
9% protein; made from Soft Summer Red Wheat

CAKE FLOUR
7-8% protein; made from Soft Summer Red Wheat

DID YOU KNOW?

- Sometimes flour is bleached by aging it or by using chemicals on it. Bleached flours are lower in protein and have fewer vitamins. Sometimes these are added back in, and the flour is labeled "enriched."

- Most commercial flours are manufactured with steel grinders, which destroys some of the vitamins.

- Stone ground flour uses a process that retains the wheat's nutrients.

- Self-rising flour has had baking powder and salt added to it.

- European flour labels indicate the grind. "00" flour is very, very fine, like baby powder. Sometimes you see "00" flour in specialty stores marked as pizza flour. "00" can be fun to experiment with, but regular Bread Flour will be fine for pasta and flatbreads.

A NOTE ABOUT FLOUR & BREAD
(continued)

THE SCIENCE OF BREAD

- Flour contains two different kinds of protein.

- When you combine flour and water it forms gluten from the protein and H_2O.

- As the dough is kneaded and stretched, it makes more gluten.

- The gluten gets long and flexible, like strands.

- The more you knead, the stronger and more elastic the gluten strands become.

- The yeast you add to bread makes carbon dioxide gas that gets trapped in the gluten strands and causes the dough to expand, like inside a balloon.

- Adding fat shortens the protein, reducing the production of gluten, which traps less gas. That's why cakes and muffins have a different texture from bread.

GETTING A RISE OUT OF IT

- Yeast is a biological leavener. The name comes from an Indo-European word meaning bubble or boil.

- Yeast is a fungus and could be the world's first cultivated organism.

- Yeast converts sugar to carbon dioxide.

- A granulated, active dry yeast was developed in North America during World War II and did not require refrigeration.

- The longer or the more times a bread is allowed to rise, the better the flavor.

- The dump, or direct method was developed using dry yeast. It does not require proofing the yeast first.

- *Poolish*, or indirect method, combines small, equal parts of flour and water with yeast, to pre-ferment before being combined with the rest of ingredients to make bread. This adds extra flavor.

- Sourdough starter is a kind of *poolish*.

- Baking soda and baking powder are chemical leaveners, commonly used when a yeast flavor is not desired, like with cookies and cakes. Baking soda is pure sodium bicarbonate and will taste bitter unless countered by acid like buttermilk. Baking powder contains 1 part baking soda plus 2 parts cream of tartar and has a neutral taste.

KITCHEN RULES

BE CLEAN

- Wash your hands with soap and water for at least 20 seconds before you start cooking.
- Make sure your nails are clean.
- Tie back long hair so it won't get in your way or fall into your dish.
- Take off any jewelry you are wearing on your hands.
- Wear an apron.
- Roll up and secure long sleeves.
- Clear and clean a work area.
- Clean up spills as they happen.
- Use a different knife and cutting board for meat than you do for fruits and vegetables.
- Wash your hands again after handling meat, chicken or fresh eggs.
- Clean your workspace and all your equipment after you finish cooking.

BE CAREFUL

- Ask an adult's help if you plan to use electric equipment or fire.
- Always read the recipe from beginning to end **before** you start cooking.
- Collect and measure all of your ingredients to create a *mise en place*, which is French for "putting things out in order."
- Pay attention to the recipe and follow instructions, especially when you make something for the first time. You can get creative later—swapping out ingredients, changing measurements, substituting—once you know how the dish was originally intended to taste.
- Stay calm and focused.
- Never run in the kitchen.
- Don't touch hot pots and pans without wearing an oven mitt or using a potholder.
- Don't touch anything electric when your hands are wet.
- Be especially careful with knives and sharp objects.
- Wear oven mitts whenever you open the oven or broiler and work with food inside the oven.
- Keep handles of pots and pans turned to the side when they are on the stove.
- Make sure you have turned everything off when you finish.
- Know when to ask for help and don't be embarrassed or afraid to.

Be a food adventurer and try everything, even thinking of new ways to adapt recipes and make them your special signature dish.

HOW MUCH IS THIS?

MISCELLANEOUS

1 pinch	=	$\frac{1}{16}$ teaspoon or less of a dry ingredient
1 teaspoon	=	60 drops
1 dash	=	$\frac{1}{16}$ teaspoon or less of a liquid ingredient

LIQUID MEASUREMENTS

In the United States, liquid measurement is not only used for liquids such as water and milk, it is also used when measuring other ingredients such as flour, sugar, shortening, butter, and spices. Our most common use is in **BOLD.**

	teaspoon	tablespoon	fluid ounce	cup	pint	quart	gallon
1 teaspoon =	**1**	$\frac{1}{3}$	$\frac{1}{6}$	- - -	- - -	- - -	- - -
1 tablespoon =	**3**	1	$\frac{1}{2}$	$\frac{1}{16}$	- - -	- - -	- - -
1 fluid ounce =	6	**2**	1	$\frac{1}{8}$	$\frac{1}{16}$	- - -	- - -
1 gill =	24	8	4	$\frac{1}{2}$	$\frac{1}{4}$	$\frac{1}{8}$	- - -
1 cup =	48	16	**8**	1	$\frac{1}{2}$	$\frac{1}{4}$	$\frac{1}{16}$
1 pint =	96	32	16	**2**	1	$\frac{1}{2}$	$\frac{1}{8}$
1 quart =	192	64	32	4	**2**	1	$\frac{1}{4}$
1 gallon =	768	256	128	16	8	**4**	1

KITCHEN STUFF

BLENDER

CAN OPENER

BAKING DISH

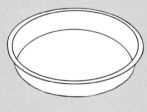

ROUND CAKE PAN

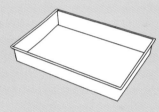

SQUARE CAKE PAN

CHEESE CLOTH

COLANDER

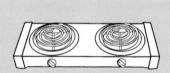

COOKTOP

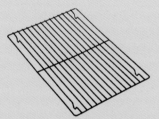

COOLING RACK

CUTTING BOARD

DUTCH OVEN

EGG BEATER

EGG SLICER

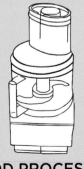

FOOD PROCESSOR

 **GRATER/BOX GRATER**

 **JUICER**

 **LARGE POT FOR PASTA**

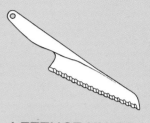 **LETTUCE KNIFE**

 **LOAF PAN**

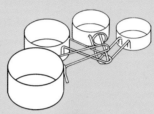 **DRY MEASURING CUPS**

 **LIQUID MEASURING CUPS**

 **MEASURING SPOONS**

 **MIXING BOWLS SMALL AND LARGE**

 **MIXING SPOON**

 **MIXER-ELECTRIC**

 **OVEN**

 **PASTA MACHINE**

 **PASTRY BRUSH**

KITCHEN STUFF *(continued)*

PEELER

MORTAR & PESTLE

MUFFIN TIN

NUT & SPICE GRINDER

PIE PAN

PIZZA PAN

ROLLING PIN

SALAD SPINNER

SAUCE PAN

SAUTE PAN

SCISSORS
FOR SNIPPING HERBS

SCRAPER

SIEVE/STRAINER

SHEET PAN/
COOKIE SHEET

SKILLET

SLOW COOKER

SPATULA

SPOONS:
SLOTTED, WOODEN,
METAL, SOUP LADLE

STEAMER

STOCK POT

TIMER

TOASTER

TOASTER OVEN

THERMOMETER

TONGS

WHISK

WOK

ZESTER

HOW DO I?

HOLD A KNIFE

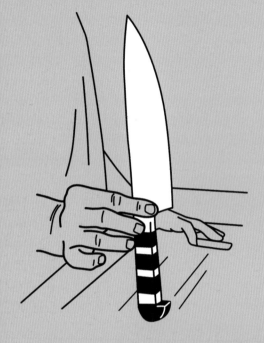

USE SAFE CUTTING TECHNIQUES

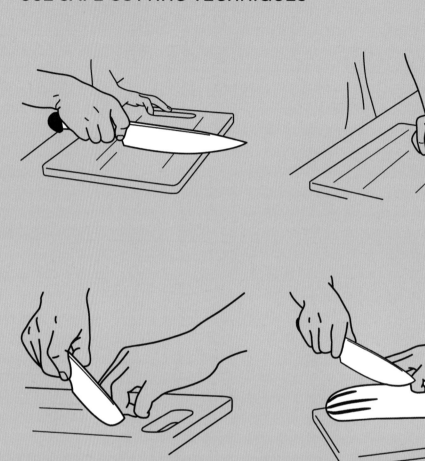

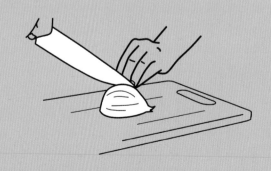

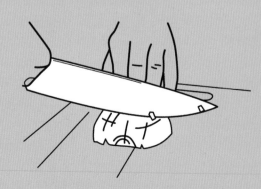

JULIENNE A BELL PEPPER

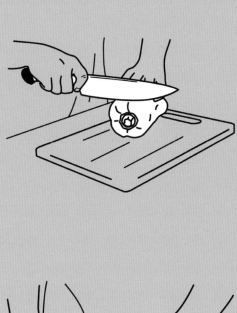 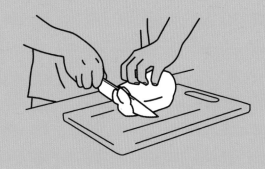 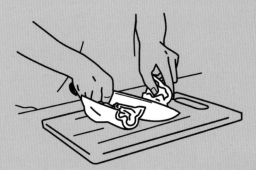

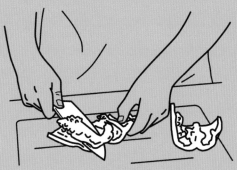 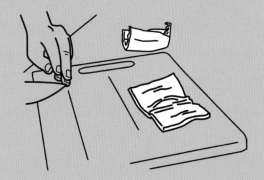 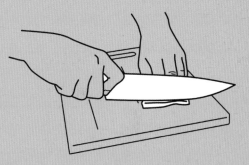

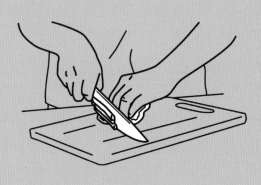 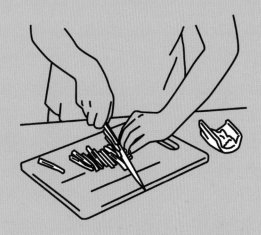

HOW DO I? *(continued)*

USE SCISSORS INSTEAD OF A KNIFE TO CUT A GREEN ONION

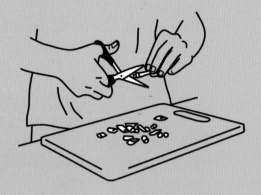

USE SCISSORS INSTEAD OF A KNIFE TO SNIP HERBS

USE A JAR CHOPPER TO CHOP OR MINCE

SEED A CUCUMBER WITH A SPOON

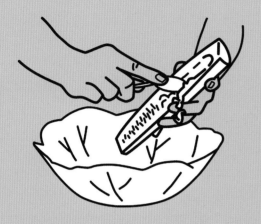

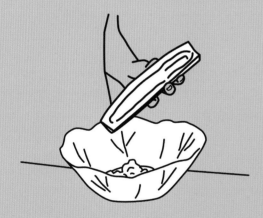

PEEL GINGER WITH SPOON

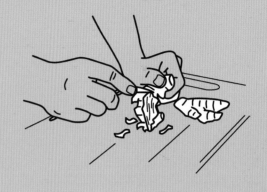

MAKE A WELL IN FLOUR

COOKING TERMS

AL DENTE
To cook pasta until it is tender but still slightly firm to the bite.

AROMATICS
An herb, spice, or vegetable that is added to food to boost the aroma or smell.

BAKE
To cook breads, pastries, vegetables or fish in the oven.

BASTE
To moisten food by brushing or spooning liquid onto it as it cooks. The liquid can be a sauce, marinade, juice, water, broth, etc.

BATTER
(*Noun*) A mixture that usually consists of flour, egg, and milk that is used for pancakes, cakes and for coating foods before frying.

(*Verb*) To cover food with batter before frying.

BEAT
To very quickly stir a mixture so as to incorporate air into it using a whisk, spoon, fork, a hand crank egg beater or by using an electric mixer.

BIND
To form a chemical bond.

BLANCH
To dip food in boiling water for a few seconds, usually to loosen the skin, brighten color or to kill enzymes.

BLEND
To mix ingredients together until they are evenly combined and won't separate.

BOIL
To heat a liquid until bubbles form on the surface.

BRAISE
To cook by browning briefly in hot oil, then adding a small amount of liquid, covering the pot, and cooking slowly at a low temperature.

BREAD
To coat food with fine crumbs made from bread, crackers, cereal, ground nuts or other dry ingredient, before cooking.

BROIL
To cook food at a high temperature with direct heat, usually from above.

BROTH
A flavorful liquid made by cooking meats and/or vegetables with herbs and water for a long time; used as a base for soup and sauces.

BROWN
To cook something until it turns brown.

BRUSH
To apply a liquid, such as melted butter or egg whites, with a pastry brush.

CARAMELIZE
To heat sugar until it turns dark brown. Some vegetables, such as onions, contain natural sugar and can be caramelized without adding additional sugar.

CHILL
Reduce temperature, often in the refrigerator, or over ice.

CHOP
To cut into pieces with a knife, jar chopper, blender, or food processor.

COATS A SPOON
When a liquid leaves a thin layer on a metal spoon.

COAT
To cover or roll food in another ingredient.

COMBINE
To join two or more ingredients to make a single substance.

CORE
To remove the fibrous central part of a fruit. Apples or pears are examples of fruits that are usually cored.

CREAM
Mixing butter, shortening or margarine with sugar until it's light and fluffy.

CRISP
Something dry and firm with a texture that breaks easily. Verb: to make something crisper, usually in the oven.

CRUSH
To grind something into tiny bits with a rolling pin or kitchen mallet.

CUBE
Cutting foods such as vegetables or meat into pieces with 6 equal sides.

CURDLE
To cause a liquid such as milk to separate into curds and whey.

CUT
To divide something into pieces using a knife or scissors.

CUT IN
Cut butter or shortening into a flour mixture, using a fork or pastry cutter, so that you are left with small distinct pieces of fat coated in flour.

DASH
Less than $\frac{1}{16}$ teaspoon of liquid, which is a tiny amount.

DEEP FRY
To cook food in a pot or pan or electric fryer. completely submerged in hot oil.

DEGLAZE
After cooking or roasting meat, adding liquid such as vinegar, broth or water to dissolve the juices stuck to the bottom of the pan. Deglazing is often used when making sauces.

DICE
To cut food into small cubes.

DILUTE
To make something thinner or weaker by adding water or another liquid to it.

DISSOLVE
To become absorbed into a liquid, for example, adding salt or sugar to water and stirring until the granules have melted into the liquid.

DOUGH
A soft, elastic mixture of flour and water, often with other ingredients like yeast, oil, eggs, salt or sugar that becomes bread or pastry when cooked.

DRAIN
To strain out all the liquid.

DREDGE
To dip food in flour, breadcrumbs or cracker crumbs to lightly coat it.

DRIPPINGS
What is left in the bottom of a baking pan after roasting meat.

COOKING TERMS *(continued)*

DRIZZLE
Pouring a liquid in a slow, light trickle.

DUST
To sprinkle something with a powdery substance.

EGG WASH
A mixture of egg yolk and water often used to coat or brush on baked goods to turn the crust a shiny brown when cooked.

ENTRÉE
In the USA, the main dish served at a meal, usually a larger serving of protein; or a small first course in Europe.

FILLET (FILET)
(*Verb*) Remove bones from fish, poultry or meat.

(*Noun*) a boneless portion cut from a fish, a poultry breast or a rib portion of meat.

FIRM BALL STAGE
When making candy, this is when boiling syrup dropped in cold water forms a ball that will give slightly when squeezed.

FLAKE
Breaking food apart with a fork usually used for fish.

FLAMBÉ
A recipe that features pouring liquor over food and lighting it on fire with a match in order to burn off the alcohol and leave just the flavor.

FLUTE
To make a decorative groove or pleat, like in the edge of a piecrust.

FOLD
To combine ingredients together carefully by dipping down through a mixture with a spoon or spatula and bringing it back up to the top gently.

FRY
To cook something in a deep layer of fat over high heat.

GARNISH
(*Verb*) To add an edible decoration to make food more attractive.

(*Noun*) the decoration used.

GEL
To let a liquid food set or become semi-solid, usually by adding gelatin.

GLAZE
To brush food with milk, egg or sugar before baking in order to give it a shiny brown appearance, or to add a thin coating to something after it is cooked.

GRATE
To shred food into tiny pieces by rubbing against a grater.

GREASE
(*Verb*) To coat or rub a pan with a thin layer of oil or shortening.

(*Noun*) Animal fat.

GRILL
To cook food over a direct open flame.

GRIND
To crush something into very small pieces with a food processor, blender, or grinder.

HULL
(*Verb*) To remove the outer rind, shell (hull) from a fruit or vegetable or the leaves from a strawberry.

ICE
To cool over ice; to cover something in icing.

INCORPORATE
To unite or combine one thing with another to form a united substance.

JUICE
To squeeze and remove all the liquid from a fruit or vegetable.

JULIENNE
To slice fruits or vegetables in long, thin segments.

KNEAD
To fold, press and stretch dough to break down proteins.

LEAVEN
Something to make dough rise such as yeast, baking soda, or baking powder.

LUKEWARM
Just slightly warm, not too hot to touch.

MARBLE
(*Verb*) To cut one color or texture into another to form a swirl pattern.

MARINATE
To soak a food in liquid in order to tenderize and/or add flavor to it.

MASH
To squash something into a smooth mass.

MERINGUE
A mixture of egg whites and sugar that is beaten until stiff, then cooked, used to make confections and top pies.

MICROWAVE
A device that cooks with electromagnetic waves rather than heat.

MINCE
To chop finely, in very small pieces.

MISE EN PLACE
To measure and prepare all the ingredients in a recipe in advance before beginning to make it. As you become a more experienced cook, you may simply gather all your ingredients together in advance, and prepare them as you go along.

MIX
To stir ingredients together using a spoon, fork or mixer until combined.

MOISTEN
To add a small amount of liquid to something.

PAN FRY
To cook in a pan or skillet at a high heat, using a small amount of fat.

PARBOIL
To boil something until it is only partly cooked.

PARCHMENT
A coated paper used often in cooking and baking.

PARE
To peel or cut away the skin or thin outer layer of something with a small knife.

PEAKS
Egg whites beaten into a stiff, pointy meringue.

PEEL
To pare or trim away the skin of fruits or vegetables using a peeler or small paring knife.

PINCH
A small amount of dry seasoning, less than $\frac{1}{16}$ teaspoon that you can hold between your thumb and forefinger.

COOKING TERMS *(continued)*

PIPE
To decorate food using a paste, forced out of a bag that has a nozzle designed to create decorative forms, or by using a small plastic bag with the corner cut out.

PIT
To remove the large center seed from a fruit such as an apricot, cherry, avocado, peach or plum.

POACH
To cook something by slowly simmering it in a small amount of liquid.

PRESSURE COOK
To steam at a high temperature using a specially sealed pot that traps the heated vapors.

PROOF
To activate yeast in warm water.

PURÉE
(*Verb*) To liquefy a food into a thick moist paste by mashing or blending it.

(*Noun*) the resulting paste.

REDUCE
To make a sauce or stock thicker by boiling off liquid.

RE-HYDRATE
To soak dried foods in liquid.

ROAST
To cook something with dry heat in an oven or over an open fire.

ROUX
A mixture of flour and fat that is cooked briefly to brown it; used to thicken sauces.

RUB
A dry mixture of ground spices used to coat meat before cooking.

SAUTÉ
(*Verb*) Cooking food quickly and lightly in a small amount of butter, oil or fat.

SCALD
To heat a liquid to just under the boiling point.

SCORE
Make shallow cuts into something.

SEAR
To cook just the outside of something, almost to the burning point, using intense heat.

SEASON
To add salt, pepper or other spices.

SET
Allowing food to cool and harden.

SHRED
To tear something into ragged strips. Two forks can be used to shred cooked meat.

SIFT
To pass a dry ingredient through a mesh strainer or flour sifter.

SIMMER
To cook gently over low heat that is set just below the boiling point.

SKEWER
A thin wood or metal reed-like stick.

SKIM
To remove substance, such as fat, that forms a top layer over a liquid.

SLICE

(Verb) To cut crosswise into thin even sections.

(Noun) Something that has been cut.

SPRINKLE

To scatter droplets of liquid or a light dusting of powder.

STEAM

To cook food in the accumulated steam of boiling water, usually in a covered pan, suspended in a basket that keeps it from touching the water.

STEEP

To soak something in liquid.

STEW

(*Verb*) Slowly simmer meat, fish and/or vegetables in liquid.

(*Noun*) The resulting dish.

STIR-FRY

Cooking cubes of meat and/or vegetables on high heat with a small amount of oil, while stirring constantly.

STIR

To move a fork or spoon in a circular motion through liquid to mix or cool it, or through dry ingredients to mix them together.

STOCK

A flavorful liquid made by cooking meat bones and/or vegetables with herbs and water for a long time; used as a base for soup and sauces.

STRAIN

To drain liquid and reserve solids.

THICKEN

To use a roux, pureed potatoes or a cornstarch and water paste to thicken a sauce or broth.

THIN

To add more liquid in order to reduce thickness.

TOAST

To heat bread or other food under a broiler, on a grill, or in a toaster until it becomes brown.

TOSS

To lightly mix ingredients together.

UNLEAVENED

Baked goods without yeast or other raising agent.

WATER BATH

To bake food in a dish that is set into a larger pan filled with water.

WHIP

To beat ingredients together quickly with a manual or electric mixer until light and fluffy.

WHISK

To use a fork, whisk or electric mixer in order to add air to something with short quick movements making it creamy or stiff.

ZEST

(*Verb*) To remove the outer rind of the peel of citrus fruit with a small grater.

(*Noun*) The thin outer rind of a citrus peel.

INDEX (continued)

1271, 20

13th Century, 76, 78, 91, 117, 118, 120, 122, 128

Acre, 35, 39, 40, 46

Adriatic Sea, 35

Afghanistan, 117

Africa, 39, 116, 118, 124

Agora, 44

Alexander the Great, 122

Alexandria, 39, 118

Alita Dolcia, 53, 122

Allan King, 92

All Purpose Flour, 129

Almonds, 80, 110, 116

Amenhotep II, 119

Anchovy, 88, 116

Aphrodite, 40, 123

Apothecary, 24

Apple(s), 112, 116

Arabic, 128

Argo Navis, 41

Aristotle, 125

Aromatics, 142

Artichoke(s), 45-46, 80, 116

ARTICHOKES & ORZO, 80

Arugula, 72

Asparagus, 24, 25, 28, 74, 82, 83, 116

ASPARAGUS RISOTTO, 82

Babylonians, 126

Bachelor Button, 94

Bake, 142

Baking Powder, 130

Baking Soda, 130

Banana, 116

Barley, 88, 116

BARLEY & LENTIL SOUP, 88

Barter, 39

Basil, 45, 72, 74, 83, 86, 117

Baste, 142

Batter, 142

Beat, 142

Belgium, 91

Bell Pepper (Red), 74, 102

Bind, 142

Black Pepper, 117

Blanch, 142

Blend, 142

Blueberries, 52

Boil, 142

Borage, 94, 114, 117

Braise, 142

Bread, 128, 142

    Ayish , 128

Bread Flour, 129

Broccoli, 74, 83, 93, 105, 117

Broil, 142

Broth, 142

Brown, 142

Brown Sugar, 117

Brush, 142

Brussels Sprouts, 90, 92, 117

Burma, 121

Buttermilk, 117

Cake Flour, 129

Canal, 20

Captain, 21, 36, 43, 45, 46

Caramelize, 142

Carnations, 94

Carrot(s), 37, 83, 88, 92, 104, 117

Catherine de Medici, 125

Cauliflower, 93, 105

Celery, 88, 104, 118

Ceylon, 24

Charcoal, 101

Chard, 104 (See Swiss Chard)

Cherries, 112, 118

Chiffonade, 74

Chill, 142

China, 18, 39, 119, 121, 122, 123, 125

Chinese, 37, 125, 126

Chop, 142

Christopher Columbus, 119

Chrysanthemums, 94

Cinnamon, 19, 24, 28, 40, 43, 70, 86, 108, 118

Coat, 143

Coats a Spoon, 142

Cod, 104, 119

Colonnes di Marco de Teodoro, 33

Combine, 143

CONFETTI PASTA, 66, 67, 78

Constantinople, 21, 39

Constellation, 128

Core, 143

Cornflower, 94

Cream, 143

Cream of Tartar, 130

Crete, 116, 119-121

Crisp, 143

Croatia, 35

Crusaders, 118

Crush, 143

Cube, 143

Cucumber(s), 98, 102, 119

Curdle, 143

Cut (in), 143

Daisy, 94

Dandelions, 94

Dash, 143

Dates, 112

Deep Fry, 143

Deglaze, 62, 81, 143

Dice, 143

Dill, 119

Dilute, 143

Dissolve, 143

Dough, 143

Drain, 143

Dredge, 143

Drippings, 143

Drizzle, 144

Drum Fish, 104

Dust, 144

Dutch, 91

Dutch East India Company, 118

Edible Flowers, 94

INDEX *(continued)*

Egg Wash, 144

Eggs, 52, 53, 66, 70, 86, 110, 119, 132, 143

Egypt, 116, 118, 119, 120, 121, 123-124

Egyptian(s), 116, 120-121, 126, 128

Emperor Charlemagne, 124

Emperor Nero, 121

Entrée, 144

Etruscans, 120

Europe, 20, 27, 116-119, 121-126, 144

European, 7, 33, 39, 129-130

Feta, 102, 119

FETA & VEGGIE ROLL UPS, 102

Figs, 110, 119

Fillet, 144

Firm Ball Stage, 144

FISH SOUP, 28, 104

Flake, 144

Flambé, 144

Flatbread, 54, 56, 60, 62, 112

      BASIC WHOLE WHEAT FLATBREAD, 54

Florentine, 125

Flute, 144

Focaccia, 29, 35-36, 41, 44, 46, 55-56, 58, 81, 120

      EASY FOCACCIA, 56

      TRADITIONAL FOCACCIA GENOVESE, 58

Fold, 144

Fork, 27

Fornero, Ottavio (Tavi), 17-46, 53, 63, 67, 72, 78, 83, 87, 89, 91, 94, 98, 105, 114

France, 119, 120, 125

FRUIT & HONEY BUNDLES, 112

Fry, 144

Fuchsia, 94

Gallant, 40

Galley, 21, 23, 24, 33, 34, 36, 39, 40, 45

Gangplank, 21, 33, 34, 44

Garlic, 36, 45-46, 62, 72-74, 76, 80, 88, 92, 95, 98, 102, 120

Garnish, 144

Gel, 144

Genoa, Italy, 29, 58, 120

Ginger, 120

Gladiators, 116

Glaze, 144

Gluten, 129

Golden Fleece, 41

Gondola, 20, 33

Gondoliers, 17, 20

Grand Canal, 21, 23, 33

Grate, 144

Grease, 144

Great Britain, 119

Greece, 43, 58, 119-121, 123

Greek(s), 13, 24, 40, 49, 96-98, 114, 116, 119-126, 128

GREEK YOGURT (HOMEMADE), 98

Green Beans, 105

Green Onion, 124

Gremolata, 93

Grill, 144

Grind, 144

Gruyere Cheese, 62, 120

Haiti, 119

Ham, 83

Hesperus, 40

Hibiscus, 94

Hippocrates, 126

Honey, 35, 45, 52-54, 73, 86, 90, 94, 95, 108, 110, 112, 114, 120

Honeysuckle, 94

Hull, 144

Ice, 144

Iliad and the Odyssey, 118

Impatiens, 94

Incorporate, 145

India, 39, 116-121, 124-125, 128

Indian Ocean, 116

Indonesia, 117, 120-121

Israel, 124

Italian Sausage, 83

Italian-style Turkey Sausage, 88

Italy, 119-122, 125-126

Jason and the Argonauts, 41

Java, 24

Jordan, 119, 123

Juice, 145

Julienne, 103, 145

KALAMAKI, 61, 98, 100

Kale, 88, 104

King Henry II, 125

Knead(ing), 66, 145

Kublai Khan, 17

Lamb, 100, 120

Lance Fegan, 102

Lasagna, See Losyns

Leaven, 145

Leavener, See Yeast

Leek, 104, 121

Lemon(s), 44, 121

Lentils, 88, 121

Lettuce, 120

Libra Denariorum Venetialium, 34

Liguria, 58

LOSYNS, 28, 43, 70

Lukewarm, 145

Malabar Coast, 117

Maffeo Polo, 29, 39, 40

Mammoni, 19

Marble, 145

Marco Polo, 8-9, 17-25, 29, 33-37, 39-41, 43-46

Marigolds, 94

Marinate, 145

Marjoram, 121

Mash, 145

Measurements, 133

Medieval, 70, 119, 122, 123

Mediterranean (Sea), 73, 116, 120-126

Meringue, 145

Mesolithic Rock Painting, 120

Microwave, 145

Middle Ages, 117, 121, 122, 124, 126, 128

Middle East(ern), 73, 116- 123, 125-126

Milk, 96

Mince, 145

Mint, 102

INDEX *(continued)*

Mise en Place, 132, 145

Mix, 145

Moisten, 145

Molo di San Marco, 33

Monica Pope, 11

Mozzarella, 19, 24, 70, 121

Mushroom(s), 25, 28, 33, 36, 62, 82, 121

RUSTIC MUSHROOM TARTS, 62

Mycenaean Greeks, 118

Narcissus, 114

Nasturtiums, 94

Negroponte, 35, 43, 44

Nepal, 125

Netherlands, 117

Niccolò Polo, 17, 20, 25, 28, 29, 33, 36, 39, 40, 46

Nile, 123

Nomads, 128

Noodles, 68

North Africa, 126

Nutmeg, 19, 24, 40, 70, 78, 82, 86, 108, 112, 121

Odyssey, 122

Olive Oil, 29, 35, 44, 46, 54, 56, 58, 59, 62, 66, 72-74, 76, 80, 82, 92, 95, 98, 100, 102, 121

Onions, 37, 121

Orecchiette, 76

Oregano, 44, 45, 70, 73, 78, 86, 88, 89, 100, 102, 121, 122

Orzo, 80

ARTICHOKES & ORZO, 80

Ottavio Fonero (Tavi), 17-46, 53, 63, 67, 72, 78, 83, 87, 89, 91, 94, 98, 105, 114

Paddlewheel, 128

Pakistan, 124

Pan Fry, 145

PANCAKES, 52, 122

Pansy, 94

Paprika, 122

Papua, New Guinea, 116

Parboil, 145

Parchment, 145

Pare, 145

Parmesan Cheese, 56, 70, 73, 74, 77, 78, 80, 82, 89, 122

Parmigiano-Reggiano Cheese, 72

Parsley, 122

Parsnips, 88, 92, 122

Pasta, 122

ARTICHOKES & ORZO, 80

CONFETTI PASTA, 66, 67, 78

BASIC FRESH PASTA DOUGH, 66

PASTA PRIMAVERA, 74

RADISHES & GREENS WITH PASTA, 76

RAVIOLI WITH FRESH HERBS, 78

Pasta Machine, 68

Pastry Flour, 129

Peaches, 111, 122

Peaks, 145

Pears, 28, 52, 108, 122, 143

PEARS & CINNAMON, 108

Peas, 74, 78, 83, 123

Peel, 145

Persia, 33, 73, 121, 122, 125

PESTO, 72, 79

Pharaoh Senusret, 120

Phoenician traders, 121

Piano Nobile, 29

Piazza San Marco, 20

Pike, 104

Pinch, 145

Pine Nuts, 46, 72, 80, 123

Pipe, 146

Pit, 146

PITA, 44, 46, 54, 55, 60, 61, 98, 101, 102, 123

Pliny the Elder, 126

Plums, 111

Poach, 146

Pondera , 24

Polo,

    Marco, 8-9, 17-25, 29, 33-37, 39-41, 43-46

    Maffeo, 29, 39, 40

    Niccolò, 17, 20, 25, 28, 29, 33, 36, 39, 40, 46

Poolish, 58, 130

Poop Deck, 21, 35, 36, 37, 40

Potatoes (Red), 104

Pressure cook, 146

Proof, 146

Purée, 146

Queen Anne's Lace, 94

Radishes, 12, 44, 49, 76, 123

RADISHES & GREENS WITH PASTA, 76

Raisins, 112

Raspberries, 123

RAVIOLI WITH FRESH HERBS, 78

Raviolis, 28

Recipe for Success Foundation, 7, 8, 9

Reduce, 146

Re-hydrate, 146

Rhodes, 24

Rialto, 20, 21, 23, 24, 40, 44

Rice, 82, 123

Ricotta, 19, 24, 62, 70, 78, 123

River Thames, 128

Roast, 146

ROASTED VEGETABLES WITH GREMOLATA, 92

Roman(s), 116-126, 128

Roman Empire, 116, 117, 120, 124

Rome, 116, 117

Rose(s), 94, 114

Rosemary, 29, 36, 56, 58, 59, 120, 123

Roux, 146

Rub, 146

Saffron, 13, 24, 40, 49, 110, 124

SAFFRON & FIG CAKE, 110

Sage, 124

Sauté, 146

Scald, 146

Scallion, 124

Score, 146

Sea of Galilee, 116

Sea salt, 124

Sear, 146

Season, 146

Seed-to-Plate Nutrition Nutrition Education, 7

Seminola, 129

INDEX (continued)

Sesame Seed, 124

Set, 146

Shallot, 124

Shish-ka-bob, 100

Shred, 146

Sicily, 116, 123

Sift, 146

Silk Road, 39

Simmer, 146

Skewer, 146

Skim, 146

Slice, 147

Sofrito, 74

Sour Cream, 124

Southeast Asia, 116, 119, 120, 121

Souvlaki, 100

Spice Route, 39, 118

Spinach, 66, 70, 74, 78, 83, 88, 104, 125

SPRING SALAD IN BLOOM, 94

Sprinkle, 147

Starflower, 94, 114

Steam, 147

Steep, 147

Stew, 147

Stir, 147

Stir-fry, 147

Stock, 147

Strain, 147

Strawberry, 125

STUFFED EGGS, 28, 86

Sumac, 45, 46, 73, 125

Sumatra, 24

Swiss Chard, 88, 125

Switzerland, 120

Syria, 117, 123

Tahini, 73, 125

Tarragon, 125

Tavi Fonero (Ottavio), 17-46, 53, 63, 67, 72, 78, 83, 87, 89, 91, 94, 98, 105, 114

Thicken, 147

Thin, 147

Thyme, 45, 62, 73, 78, 86, 104, 114, 126

Tibet, 116

Tilapia, 104

Toast, 147

Toss, 147

Tulips, 94

Turkey, 116, 118, 123

Turkish, 122, 126

Turnips, 37, 92, 126

Tutankhamen, 118

TZATZIKI, 98, 100

Unleavened, 147

Vanilla, 126

Venetian, 17-18, 20-21, 27-28, 40, 43, 45, 118

Venice, 17, 20, 24-25, 28, 33, 35-36, 39, 44, 78, 91

Vinegar, 126

Violets, 94

Wales, 121

Walnuts, 80, 90, 92, 126

WALNUTS IN BRUSSELS, 90

Water bath, 147

Wheat, 128

Whip, 147

Whisk, 147

White Pepper, 126

White Whole Wheat Flour, 129

WHOLE WHEAT FLATBREAD, 54, 56, 60, 62, 112

Whole Wheat Flour, 129

Windmill, 128

Winter Squash, 93

Yeast, 130

YIAOURTI ME MELI, 114

Yogurt, 96, 97, 108, 109, 111, 113, 114, 126

    GREEK STYLE YOGURT, 97

    HOMEMADE YOGURT, 96

ZA'ATAR, 73

Zest, 147

ABOUT THE AUTHOR

GRACIE CAVNAR

Journalist, Writer, Philanthropist
Founder & CEO, Recipe for Success Foundation

Gracie Cavnar is a lifelong cooking and gardening enthusiast. In 1998, a news item about vending machines in elementary schools caught her eye and moved her to action. While working to remove junk food from schools in Texas, she learned about the widespread epidemic of childhood obesity and the astounding affect it was having on American lives and wallets. She decided to focus her energy on turning back the tide of childhood obesity and launched Recipe for Success Foundation in 2005 to change the way children understand, appreciate and eat their food. She has received many awards and recognition for her work and grown her Seed-to-Plate Nutrition Education™ for children from a small pilot in Houston to one with national scope. She has taught tens of thousands of children that growing and cooking their own healthy food can be easy, tasty and fun—an adventure!

Gracie donates her time as CEO of the Foundation while she continues to write news articles, feature stories, editorials and to blog. *Eat It! Food Adventures with Marco Polo* is her first children's book.

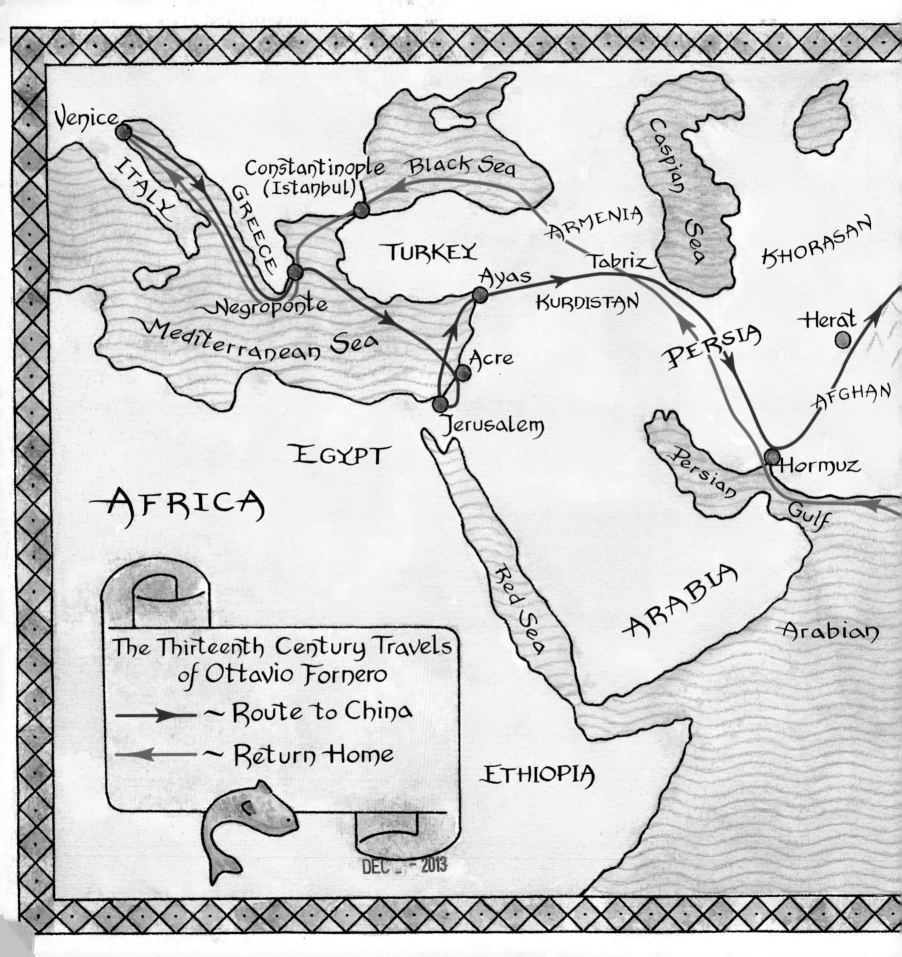

Venice

ITALY

GREECE

Constantinople
(Istanbul)

Black Sea

TURKEY

Caspian Sea

KHORASAN

ARMENIA

Tabriz

Ayas

KURDISTAN

PERSIA

Herat

Negroponte

AFGHAN

Mediterranean Sea

Acre

Jerusalem

EGYPT

AFRICA

Persian Gulf

Hormuz

Red Sea

ARABIA

Arabian

The Thirteenth Century Travels
of Ottavio Fornero

→ ~ Route to China

← ~ Return Home

ETHIOPIA

DEC - 2013